TALES FROM THE DUGOUT

TALES FROM THE DUGOUT

FOOTBALL AT THE SHARP END

RICHARD GORDON

BLACK & WHITE PUBLISHING

First published 2015
by Black & White Publishing Ltd
29 Ocean Drive, Edinburgh EH6 6JL

1 3 5 7 9 10 8 6 4 2   15 16 17 18

ISBN 978 1 84502 989 0

A CIP catalogue record for this book is available from the British Library.

Typeset by Iolaire Typesetting, Newtonmore
Printed and bound by Gutenberg, Malta

'It was incredible, just forty-five seconds of madness.'

BILLY DODDS

'I thought I was having an embolism, I was dizzy, my brain almost popped.'

MARK McGHEE

'I've been involved in so many incidents in the dugout ... I'm ashamed of what I've done on occasion.'

BILLY BROWN

'Dugouts are a breeding ground for conflict.'

CRAIG BROWN

This book is dedicated to those who populate the area in and around the dugouts and whose antics and behaviour so often prompt the question 'Fit ye deein?'

CONTENTS

INTRODUCTION   ix

CHAPTER ONE   CRAIG BROWN   1

CHAPTER TWO   TALES FROM THE DUGOUT 1   16

CHAPTER THREE   KENNY CLARK   44

CHAPTER FOUR   TALES FROM THE DUGOUT 2   56

CHAPTER FIVE   CHICK YOUNG   84

CHAPTER SIX   TALES FROM THE DUGOUT 3   91

CHAPTER SEVEN   GORDON STRACHAN   119

CHAPTER EIGHT   TALES FROM THE DUGOUT 4   136

CHAPTER NINE   PAT NEVIN   163

CHAPTER TEN   TALES AWAY FROM THE DUGOUT   175

ACKNOWLEDGEMENTS   205

REFERENCE MATERIAL   207

INTRODUCTION

Donald Colman was a late starter in professional football, his career not really beginning properly until he signed for Aberdeen FC in 1907 at the age of twenty-nine. He played almost 350 matches for the Dons, establishing himself as a tough tackling full-back, and even won international honours, the first of his four Scotland caps being collected when he was thirty-three.

Like many of his generation, his career was interrupted by the First World War, and after serving in France, Colman wound down his time with Aberdeen before moving to Dumbarton where he developed a deep interest in the coaching side of the game.

That intensified during summer trips to Norway where he worked with local players trying to improve their standards, and in 1931 he was brought back to Pittodrie Stadium by manager Paddy Travers.

Colman was seen as something of a visionary, and was credited with heavily influencing the development of forwards Willie Mills and Matt Armstrong who would go on to forge one of the most prolific strike-force partnerships in the history of Scottish football.

He would devote long hours working with the players, focusing on movement and possession of the ball. He became obsessed with their footwork, and it was that which led him to devise the innovation which has provided countless controversies and drama, humour and a catalogue of ridiculous incidents in the years since.

He ordered the Pittodrie ground staff to dig out a sunken sheltered area by the side of the pitch from which he believed he could better study players' movements, and assess how they were performing. It allowed him to get closer to the action and to take copious notes on what he was watching, without giving up entirely the relative comforts offered by sitting in the grandstand.

In fact, the initial concept was borne out of those summer stints in Norway where coaches would stand in open-fronted huts sheltering from the weather. Colman remembered that and refined the idea, and within a few years it was one being replicated at football grounds all over the country and further afield.

Initially the structures were fairly rudimentary and for many years adhered to Colman's original basic design. They were small and had uncomfortable bench seating, but served their purpose as they housed only the coach and/or trainer – who doubled-up as 'physio' and whose full kit comprised of a bucket of water and a sponge – and on occasions the team manager. It was not until the mid 1960s that one substitute could be named; that individual claiming a further place in the dugout.

Around that time the legendary Liverpool manager Bill Shankly decided his pitchside home required refurbishment and expansion, and in typical fashion, set about doing it himself. His assistant, Bob Paisley, had apparently done a bit of bricklaying, so he was drafted in to help, along with the reserve team coach, Joe Fagan. The new dugout, constructed by the then current Liverpool boss and two men who would follow him into the Anfield hot seat, lasted for almost three decades before finally having to be replaced.

That was partly down to changes in the laws of the game

which saw more and more substitutions permitted and match day squad sizes expanding, allied to the trend for assistant managers to be appointed, and the introduction of fully qualified physiotherapists. The dugout soon became a cramped space and had to be amended accordingly.

At some stadiums this meant two rows of seats, at others plastic bucket seats were simply arranged along the wall of the main stand to cope with the growing numbers now assembling there.

There was a move away from the dugout being sunken, instead it was at pitch level, and in more recent times, where space permitted, Perspex structures were installed. At some grounds sections of the stand have been sacrificed to allow those permitted to populate the dugout to spread out more easily, while a number of clubs now boast state of the art padded seats allowing the incumbents to relax in comfort and style.

There are guidelines which must be adhered to, FIFA stipulating that while the technical area might vary in size it must clearly be marked by a white line, cannot extend more than one metre beyond the ends of the designated seated area, and has to be at least one metre away from the touchline. At some grounds that represents a fairly small area, at others it is pretty extensive, but whatever the square meterage the capacity for madness and mayhem remains much the same.

The introduction of the fourth official, a further assistant to the referee who stands between the technical areas, might have been seen as a potential for calm, an authoritative figure who could suppress potential flare-ups. It has in fact, in countless cases, had the reverse effect with that official being identified as a target, an extension of the man in the middle to whom abuse and complaints can and will be directed at the first given opportunity. The assistant referee, or linesman, on the dugout side is also seen as fair game and will regularly be pounced upon whenever he follows play up to the halfway line.

For the bigger matches, up to twenty-three people must be

accommodated within each seating area, and that means it is not just the managers and coaches who get involved. There have been many instances of physios and substitutes losing control, leading to clashes with the opposition, officialdom and even nearby supporters.

There have been a number of high profile technical area bust-ups, cock-ups and confusions, and one which falls into the latter category has gone down in the annals of the game. In January 1999 Ron Atkinson had been holidaying in Barbados when he got an emergency call to take over the vacant managerial post at Nottingham Forest. He flew in overnight, got fixed up with a club suit and overcoat, and was rushed to the City Ground. He walked out, still in a daze, to the acclaim of the crowd, paused for the photographers to get their pictures of him waving to the Forest fans, then jumped into the dugout. The wrong dugout. He turned to see the Arsenal players Dennis Bergkamp, Patrick Vieira and Nelson Vivas standing alongside him and quick as a flash delivered the immortal line, 'How can we be bottom of the league with these players in the team?'

In May 2014, during a comfortable 3–0 win over Aston Villa, the then Tottenham Hotspur boss Tim Sherwood vacated his place in the dugout, handing it over to a loudmouth fan who had been giving him stick. 'That guy sits up there every week I'm here, and he's telling me: "Get him off he's rubbish, he's an embarrassment, he's this, he's that",' the manager revealed. 'So I invited him down to show what he can do. He half-bottled it at first but in the end he took it up.' The supporter, 'Danny', later told the BBC's 606 show:

'It was great humour from him [Sherwood]. Our season tickets are there so we sit near him every week. To be fair to him he's not frightened to talk with the fans and all season we've had good banter with him. He's always happy to chat. During the game I called some substitutions that I thought he should make and it just so happened he went on to make them. Suddenly he said: "You know what? You might as well sit in the hot seat". So I thought, why not? It was just surreal I didn't know what to make of it. I didn't know if I'd get in trouble for going over the barriers.'

As the fan took his place in the technical area, Sherwood slipped off his trademark gilet and helped his replacement put it on. 'As I was walking away afterwards, Tim said: "You can keep the jacket mate." He then shook my hand and patted me on the back.'

Somewhat less well known is a story related by Mark McGhee which had been passed on by Kevin Dillon, one-time assistant manager to Steve Coppell at Reading. As often as he could, Coppell liked to watch games from the main stand and would leave his seat a few minutes before the half-time or full-time whistle. On one occasion at Preston, with his team trailing 1–0, the manager did just that, but while he was making his way down to the dressing room, and buried away inside the stadium, Reading equalised without him realising. He did his half-time team-talk and the game resumed. With ten minutes left, and Coppell now in the dugout, he was urging his players forward, demanding his full-backs push up the wings, telling his centre-halfs to get up into the box, all of which was entirely against his normal approach. Dillon was somewhat taken aback and leaned towards Coppell to ask him what he thought the score was. "We're 1–0 down . . ." Dillon grinned, "Nope, it's 1–1." At which point Coppell raced to the touchline and started screaming, "Get back, get back!"

It is not just at the big high-profile occasions that such instances occur, and the weird and wonderful can unfold wherever football is staged, as is evidenced by the case of the Italian amateur player who was sent off for headbutting his team's own dugout. It was a game between Ponticelli and Riolo Terme in the lower leagues, and after the home goalkeeper had fumbled a long-range free-kick the visiting striker scrambled it over the line. Reacting as if he had just fired a thirty-yard volley into the top corner to win the World Cup final, the player peeled away in celebration, ran halfway back along the pitch and took a diving header through the side of the Perspex dugout, landing sprawled across the thankfully empty seats. His reward? A red card brandished by a clearly stunned referee.

There are countless video clips available online which show the humour and madness which can occur in the dugout. One of the funniest involves Sir Alex Ferguson who's intently watching the match and doesn't see his assistant, Mike Phelan, catch a balloon which is floating past. When Phelan pulls it into the dugout and stamps on it, Ferguson just about jumps out of his seat in fright, turns to his number two, and bellows, "Fuck off!" Another shows Arsene Wenger fully concentrated during a game at Fulham. He has one hand in his jacket pocket and tries half a dozen times to shove the other one into the other pocket, only to keep missing it. Eventually he gives up, turns, and sits down on his seat again.

The dugout can also offer glimpses of the intense emotions the game brings to its inhabitants. There are countless scenes of celebration, of managers and coaches in that split-second of euphoria reacting to a goal or the final whistle which heralds an important victory. At the other end of the spectrum, we can all recall the crestfallen and the vanquished, and no picture better sums that up than the distraught Ally MacLeod during the ill-fated 1978 World Cup finals in Argentina. The ebullient MacLeod had boasted that Scotland would return home with the trophy, but an opening defeat to Peru was followed up by a 1–1 draw against Iran, and towards the end of that second match the camera panned to the Scots dugout. There sat a broken man, head buried in his hands, his hopes and dreams torn apart. It remains one of the saddest images in Scottish football history.

Passions of all kind spill over in the technical area. One such instance occurred in February of 2015 involving the Leicester City manager, Nigel Pearson, and Crystal Palace's Scotland midfielder, James McArthur. The Crystal Palace player had been knocked off the pitch by an opponent, and as he slid along the surface he upended Pearson, who reacted by grabbing him by the throat as he lay in front of the dugout. Pearson was under considerable pressure at the time with Leicester embroiled in a relegation battle – which they would later survive – but at that point in the campaign, with much speculation about his future, it may have been a tipping point for him. McArthur later laughed off the incident: 'These things happen in football. He says it was only a joke. I did not know that at the time but he said it was a joke so I will take it that way and move on.' Pearson endured a torrid weekend and the Leicester board was forced to issue a statement denying he had been sacked. By the end of the season the team had preserved their Premiership status, the manager's job was safe – at least for the time being; he was axed later that summer – and the altercation a fading memory, but it was a further indication that anything can happen in that high-pressure area of any football stadium at any time. These little cameos occur week-in, week-out at grounds all across the world. There are minor skirmishes, disagreements, confrontations, controversies and amusing incidents, many of which go unreported and unseen by the public at large. Among them, the story I was told by a former Motherwell player – who prefers to remain anonymous – about his ex-manager, Jim Gannon. Whenever the team scored from a routine they had worked on during training Gannon would pat himself on the back in the dugout and say, "Well done me", a move which didn't exactly endear him to his playing staff! One better known tale involves the eccentric Partick Thistle boss, John Lambie. One of his players, Colin McGlashan, went down after a hefty collision and was suffering from concussion after taking a head knock. When the physio sent word back that McGlashan was struggling and didn't know who he was, Lambie bellowed from the dugout, "Tell him he's Pele and get him back out there!"

Inevitably there were anecdotes which I cannot retell in full, either because the interviewee in question prefers not to have them aired, or they would be difficult to fully substantiate. Those include the one about the international footballer who refused to go on as a second half substitute in a vital match for his country because he was sulking at having not been selected to start the match, and various accounts of physical bust-ups in technical areas and dressing rooms.

Thankfully, there are countless stories and insights which can be told, and it is those 'Tales From The Dugout' that can be revealed, many for the first time, in the pages that follow.

CHAPTER ONE

CRAIG BROWN

There are few people in the game who have amassed the experiences of the legendary Craig Brown who has been patrolling technical areas across the world for much of the past half century as coach, assistant and manager.

After his playing career was cut short in his late-twenties by a succession of knee injuries, Craig developed his interest in coaching, and after working briefly with Ian St John, then as assistant to Willie McLean at Motherwell for a few years, secured his first managerial post when taking over from Billy McNeill as manager of Clyde in 1977.

Combining his duties with his full-time job as a teacher and lecturer, Brown led the club to the Second Division Championship title in his first season, and helped to produce young talent like Pat Nevin and Ian Ferguson during his decade in charge.

His efforts did not go unnoticed by the Scottish FA and he was appointed assistant manager to Andy Roxburgh with the national team, while at the same time overseeing the development of the youth set-up. He coached the under-16s to the World Championship final – losing out to Saudi Arabia on penalties at Hampden – and the under-21s to the semi-finals of the 1992 European Championship, where they suffered a 1–0 aggregate defeat to a strong Swedish side.

The following year he replaced Roxburgh in the top job, and led his country to both the 1996 European Championship finals and the World Cup finals in France two years later, the last time Scotland qualified for a major event at time of writing.

After resigning in 2001, he returned to club management with Preston, and later had spells as a football consultant with both Fulham and Derby County, before taking the reins at Fir Park for a highly successful year in charge of Motherwell. He was then lured north by Aberdeen, and stabilised the club at a time when a first relegation in its history seemed a distinct possibility.

He announced his retirement in March 2013 and was replaced by Derek McInnes for the post-split fixtures, but such was the impact he had made at Pittodrie, the Dons invited him to retain his link with the club in a role as non-executive director.

During his time in the game, Craig mingled with some of the biggest names in football management, could count many as close personal friends, and worked with some genuinely world-class players.

He rarely, if ever, courted controversy, preferring in his own understated way to get his message across how and when he needed to, but he was not above doing whatever was required to defend his players or team, or to get the right result. His calm, courteous approach hid a steely determination, but that will to win always lurked close to the surface under his quiet public demeanour, and led to occasional dugout bust-ups and confrontations, as well as numerous comical moments.

Craig Brown is consumed by football, is one of the game's deepest thinkers, and among his hallmarks is his attention to detail, whether it be his assessment of the opposition before and during a match, his own side's tactics, the warm-up, or the psychological mind games that can help to determine the outcome of any encounter.

That approach extends to the technical area, and the stadium set-up in general.

'All referees use what they call the right-wing diagonal, just think of any match and envisage where the linesmen are in relation to the ref. At Aberdeen for instance, there's one linesman who patrols from the away dugout to the corner flag while the other has the line in front of the away supporters. That's all wrong. When Jose Mourinho went to Chelsea the first thing he did was to move the visiting fans so they couldn't influence the assistant, and the second was to move the home dugout so that he, and not the opposition manager, had ready access to the linesman. I first picked up on this at Preston, Davie Moyes did the same thing there so that he had the advantage, and I realised the position of the dugout really is very important. I've travelled around quite a bit watching matches, and I always look out for that. I went to Lyon when Gerard Houllier was in charge there and I noticed the position the dugouts were laid out in meant that the opposing manager was just a few steps away from the linesman and he was giving him pelters throughout, so afterwards I asked him why and he said, "I was always getting into trouble, so I deliberately had them switched so I wasn't tempted to shout at the linesman and get sent off." That was an unusual twist, but I could understand his thinking.

'I spoke to Gordon Strachan when he was at Celtic – it's the same set-up there – and I asked why the Celtic manager didn't have the more advantageous dugout, and he said it was down to tradition; Jock Stein stood there, so every other manager will do the same. I posed the question when I took over at Pittodrie and got a similar response – that's where Alex Ferguson sat or stood. Had I pushed it, I could have changed it, but I didn't want to rock the boat and I could understand that thinking, that acknowledgement of the past.

'When I was the Scotland manager and they were redoing

Hampden the architect came to me and asked what I'd like and I told him I wanted the stadium to have the most futuristic dugouts ever. There's really no need for all the substitutes to be in them, they could be housed nearby, so my plan was for the dugouts to be big enough to hold only four or five people and I wanted them either on hydraulic legs or to be suspended from the stadium roof. They only needed to be about ten feet above the track, and could be lowered at the press of a button, but they would allow you still to be close enough to the action while offering a better overview of the pitch. The architect took the proposal to the then Chief Executive Jim Farry, who I liked, but he wasn't having any of it because it would block the view of some of the fans. I never believed that was a major problem, you would just have needed to lean a bit to either side and you'd see fine, and I still believe it would be an excellent idea. In fact when Aberdeen get their new stadium I'll be suggesting that very thing to the Chairman!

'What they did at Hampden was put the dugouts way back and used the lower part of the stand, and that was partly down to my stupidity, I should have stopped that. It actually cost us in a game, the World Cup qualifier against Belgium in March 2001. We were 2–0 up and they were down to ten men. They got a goal back, but we were still leading late on, and at that point, had I been right down on the touchline I'd have been making staged substitutions, breaking the play up, doing anything it took to prevent them from equalising, but because I was up in the stand and unable to have that direct influence, they went and scored in stoppage time.

'The positioning of the dugouts can also be a real inconvenience, particularly at grounds like Fulham and the old Brighton one, the Withdean, where you actually have to walk across the pitch to get to them. When I was with Preston I got sent off at Brighton one day. That was bad enough, but I then had to 'walk the plank' all the way round the track getting absolute dog's abuse from the home fans. Normally you can just nip up the tunnel, but there was no hiding place that day, and it got worse. I finally get to the directors' box and the steward tells me there's no seat for me, that I'll just have to stand, and the only place is behind a metal grille, so I'm standing there watching the game with my fingers on one of the bars, peeping through the gap. We'd been 1–0 up and we score a second late on and their directors get up and leave, so I shout across to this steward, "There's plenty fucking seats now, am I getting one?" Inevitably, one of the photographers had spotted where I was and there was a picture of me in the local paper, and it looked as if I was in jail. Next away game, the players have got a copy and blown it up and they've stuck it up on the front window of the team coach with the slogan THIS MAN IS INNOCENT.

'You also have the stadiums where the tunnel is in the corner and you have that walk along the track to the dugouts, and I don't like that. As an away manager at for instance Tannadice – Airdrie's old Broomfield was another – you're getting the abuse from the home supporters, and when I was in charge of Aberdeen, if things weren't going well, you're getting all the shouting and stick from your own fans when you're making that walk at half-time or at the end of the game. At least if the dugouts are either side of the tunnel, it's a quick handshake with the opposition and then you can disappear.

'Another ground where the positioning is unusual is Glebe Park, Brechin, where the away one is halfway down the pitch towards the eighteen yard box and right in front of the main stand and directors' box. We went there with Motherwell, a League Cup tie early in 2010–11, and I took one look at it and thought no way, I'm going to sit in the stand. Archie (Knox, Craig's assistant manager) wasn't having any of that, he says he's staying with the players, so that's how we set up, him in the dugout and me sitting up there where I got a better overall view. It was a lovely night, nice and warm, there's a decent Motherwell following, and the stand is full, lots of women there and families. Now, Archie always had this thing about the young full-back Steven Saunders and if Steven was on the far side he was an international player, but if he was on Archie's side he was shitting himself because all you heard was the constant shouting, "Saunders! Fucking Saunders!"

'This particular night Archie could hardly be closer to the boy, who's playing right-back, and I've heard him already have a couple of blasts from the dugout, and Saunders is a bag of nerves. We get a throw-in and I'm in the front row of the stand. Steven comes across to take it and I lean over and shout on him, he turns, and I tell him, "He really loves you, you know," which defuses things a little and he has a smile. At half-time I deliberately kept talking right up until the referee called the players out again, and Archie's fizzing because that meant he couldn't have a go at Saunders then. He's still fuming when the game gets underway again and early on Steven makes a mistake away across on the far side, and Archie turns from the dugout and screams up to me in the stand, "Haw Broon! See if that bastard Saunders is playing on Saturday, I'll not be there!" I swear all of Brechin must have heard him, and the whole of the stand burst out laughing.

'Everyone will remember the Euro 96 game against England. We're 1–0 down and we get a penalty. Now, the layout of the dugouts at the old Wembley was such that you could see very clearly into the opposition one, and we can see Terry Venables and Don Howe are getting ready to take off Paul Gascoigne, we can see the board with his number and they're getting the substitute ready, and I'm thinking 'yes!' I'm envisaging us about to equalise and them about to take off their best, most dangerous player. What happens? David Seaman saves Gary McAllister's kick and they go straight up the pitch and Gazza scores that fantastic goal. It was an unbelievable turn of events.

'That rebounded on us, but it might just have given us a little advantage, and that was another reminder of just how important the layout and positioning of the dugouts can be to a football manager.

'Another important aspect is how you handle the bench, what kind of rules and protocols you have. When I was playing there were no substitutes, so the dugout consisted of the manager, his assistant – if he had one – and the physio. Substitutes were introduced and the numbers grew over the years to the point now where for a World Cup match you've got a dozen potential replacements, in fact there are more people on the bench than there are on the park, so you can have a management problem. One of the biggest concerns you can have is a sulking substitute. I only had it a few times, but the worst was when I was in charge of the Scotland under-21s. Kevin Gallacher scored a great goal, a fantastic goal, in Bulgaria and I turned to the bench and everyone is up celebrating apart from one player, a striker, who shall remain nameless, but who clearly thought he should be playing and was sitting with his arms folded and a face like thunder. I went across to him, leant in, and said, "Don't you ever look for your name again in a Scotland squad" and I never picked him again. That was totally unacceptable, the demeanour of the players on the bench is really important, and feeds into the whole team spirit.

'I was at Euro 2000 working for the BBC and was covering the Italy v Romania quarter-final, and the big headline news before the match was that Alessandro Del Piero had been dropped and his place taken by a promising young player by the name of Francesco Totti. Our commentary position was right behind the Italian dugout and would you believe it, Totti scores the opening goal, and I immediately look down to the bench. The first player out of his seat, punching the air and celebrating? Del Piero. That's the kind of attitude you need in the technical area, and in the squad.

'Another, slightly different, example is from when I was at Fulham and working alongside their manager, Chris Coleman. We'd won 2–1 at Newcastle, I wasn't at the game, but he called me afterwards from the team bus and was complaining about one of our players. The guy in question – whose blushes I'll spare – had been subbed off, wasn't happy, and stormed past the dugout, never shook anyone's hand, and was straight up the tunnel pulling off his jersey. Chris was furious about this lack of respect, so followed him, and when he got to the dressing room the player had his shirt over his head in the process of taking it off, so without saying a word, he punched him in the stomach, and when he fell to the floor he gave him a boot. Chris asked me what I'd have done under those circumstances, and I told him, "See if I was your size Chris, I'd have done the same thing." I went on to ask if he had a substitution policy, advising that there needs to be clarity under such circumstances, and I offered to address the players at the training ground the following week, which I did, and began by asking the question, "How many reasons are there for substituting a player?" There was a flip chart and I got one of the guys, Carlos Bocanegra, to write them down as the suggestions came through. In the end, we came up with eleven, and they were:

- Tactical
- Injury
- Disobedience – ignoring the manager's instructions
- Risk of second yellow card and a sending-off
- To introduce a new or young player to the first team
- To run the clock down at the end of a game
- To receive acknowledgement of the crowd after, for instance, a particularly impressive performance
- Ahead of a penalty shoot-out, to bring on a specialist taker
- Ahead of a penalty shoot-out to bring on a shot-stopping goalkeeper
- Poor performance
- Squad bonus – to secure a player an additional bonus paid only if he takes to the pitch.

'The point I was trying to make was that although a player might often have an idea as to why he's been subbed, he won't always know for sure, that it's important to observe dugout etiquette, and shaking hands with the player being introduced should be viewed as paramount. I told them they should never expect the manager to shake their hand though. If a player has had to be subbed because of disobedience, for instance, their boss is hardly likely to be of a mind to publicly acknowledge them in that way, so to be consistent I never did shake a player's hand when he was coming off.

'The other thing I impressed upon the players was that they should never discuss the game once they'd been subbed and were back on the bench. It's too easy for them to start criticising some of the guys who've been left on, or the manager for making the decision, and that's the last thing you need to hear when you're in the technical area trying to direct things, an unhappy player mumping and moaning about what you've just done. I told them to talk about the weather, about their holidays, anything but the match; the dugout is incendiary enough without a guy sounding off and adding to the mix unnecessarily.

'The final point in the list of reasons that came up is an important one too, and good for morale. I remember one game up at Aberdeen when I was with Motherwell, we were cruising it, 3–0 up late on, and I turned round in the dugout and saw two young lads, Jamie Murphy and Bob McHugh, sitting there, so I said to Archie we'd put them on. He wasn't too keen, still worrying about letting anything go, but we went ahead and those boys got an extra £300 in their wage packets that week. The looks on their faces – you'd have thought we'd given them a lottery win!

'Technology has moved on of course during my time in the game; there's sometimes twenty-three cameras at a televised match these days, so that has to have a bearing on how everyone behaves in the dugout. Step out of line, and you can be sure your actions will be picked up by one of them. It can be an advantage

9

too though. Chris Coleman had a feed of the game on a television screen in his dugout at Fulham which was on a seven second delay, so if there was a contentious incident he could nip in, have a look, and then challenge the linesman or referee with confidence. And of course you see many assistant managers or coaches with an iPad in the dugout now which they use for tactical reasons, to point out to a substitute who's going on who he should be picking up at corners or free kicks for instance, or about positioning generally during the match.

'One thing that hasn't changed at all over the years is that the dugouts are a breeding ground for conflict. I've lost it on occasion, and I've seen so many of my fellow managers do likewise. Sane, rational men who just blow up at the slightest thing, all because of the pressure down there. Billy Davies is a great example; during the ninety minutes he wants to take on the world. You talk about conflict? Wee Billy is the master. When I was with him at Preston I'd get involved in occasional arguments, then step back, but Billy just couldn't help himself, and I saw him toe-to-toe, nose-to-nose with the likes of Alan Pardew, Neil Warnock, everyone in fact, and if it's not the opposing manager, it's the fourth official or linesman who's getting it. The dugout is certainly a form of entertainment when wee Billy is in it.

'I did get more involved when I was younger, and when I was Clyde boss I'd regularly have set-tos with the Queen's Park coach, Eddie Hunter. In the main it was good-natured banter, but it sometimes spilled over, and one day at Shawfield we came to blows over a throw-in. He thought it was his, I thought it was ours, and we both reached for the ball. It ended up with us rolling around on the wee banking at the side of the pitch and all the fans round about killing themselves laughing.

'Much later on in my career there were still little flashpoints. When I was Motherwell boss we were playing the Danish side Odense at Fir Park in the second leg of a European tie and they won that game to go through on aggregate, but during the match there was a penalty shout for them, and one of their directors came charging down the stairs and into the technical area screaming abuse. For some reason, he barged into me because the ref hadn't given them a penalty, I couldn't believe it, and so it was instinctive, I turned, saw his stomach there, and punched him.

'There was another incident at the end of that tunnel, and it was after I became Aberdeen manager. Now, I like the then Motherwell chairman John Boyle, because he's a character, and I used to get on well with him, but the relationship had soured after I left. There's a backstory, which I don't really want to get into, but it revolved around bonuses for the players, and money I was due, and that fed into what happened that particular afternoon. John hadn't even been at the game, he'd been off out somewhere, but I gather he'd left word that he should be called should Motherwell look like winning the game, which they did. When he arrived it appeared that he'd been drinking. I'd congratulated Stuart McCall and I turned to do the same to John, when he grabbed me, lurched into me and slavered down my face. He said something, I didn't catch what, then turned to walk away, and I chased after him and grappled with him for a moment or two before various people stepped in and separated us. He was just trying to be smart, and given the situation which had been going on in the background, it riled me and I reacted. I should have known better, but lost it in the heat of the moment.

'Those were two unsavoury incidents, but there have been very many amusing and unusual ones over the years.

'One day at Cliftonhill, Albion Rovers against Clyde, I'm in the away dugout and the Celtic legend, Harry Hood, is the Rovers manager. Midway through the second half Tam Fagan, who was the owner of Albion Rovers, suddenly came down to their dugout, he and Harry had a disagreement, and Harry just walked off, got in his car and drove home. He just left the chairman to get on with it, and was never seen again as Rovers manager.

'We were at Kirkcaldy one time, Clyde against Raith Rovers, and I'm getting pelters from the fans behind the dugout. One guy in particular is giving it plenty, and he shouts, "This is fucking shite Broon, fucking shite. The worst game I've ever seen." So, I turn to him and shout across, "You're the mug pal, you paid to get in." Quick as a flash I hear this gruff voice from the other dugout, it's Frank Connor, the Raith boss, and he calls over, "Aye, and if this carries on Broon, you'll be fucking paying in next season."

'I had signed Joe Filippi from Celtic, the biggest fee I ever paid as Clyde manager, £5,000 – three for Celtic, two for him – and we were playing against Ayr one day, one of his former clubs, and he's whacked their winger. The referee was big Davie Syme, and I know Joe is in trouble. He's a lovely big guy, a gentleman off the park, but an animal on it, and I shout over from the dugout to remind him to be polite and courteous to the referee, in the hope that the ref might be lenient with him. So Davie asks for his name, and Joe, in the full knowledge that he had a somewhat unusual surname, says, "Joseph Filippi, Mr Syme, that's Filippi with two Ps." Without even looking up from writing in his notebook, Davie replies, "Mr Filippi with two Ps, for you it's off with two Fs."

'There was the time against Raith when they were given a goal that was miles offside. I was having a moan and the referee, George Smith, came across to the dugout to calm me down and he said, "Sorry Craig, that's one I owe you." He wasn't being serious of course, but a few weeks later we were playing Airdrie at the old Broomfield and George came into the dressing room to inspect the players' boots. I reminded him that he owed me one, and he said, "I'll give you a penalty, how about midway through the second half?" He was joking of course, we had a laugh, and as we made our way along the track to the dugouts, I told the Airdrie boss, Ally MacLeod, that we'd be getting a penalty at the appropriate moment. We reach that point in the game and they're giving us a doing, they're 2–0 up and we haven't had a shot on goal. Ally turns to me and shouts across, "Haw Broon, if you're wanting that penalty, had you not better try getting some of your players into our box?"

'When I was the Motherwell assistant manager to Willie McLean, we were up at Brora in a pre-season friendly and our full-back Billy Dickson, who was a smashing player and had won a few Scotland caps, was having a shocker. Willie decides to take him off, so rather than come running across to the dugout, Billy just leaves the park on the far side and saunters round. When he gets to the bench, he sits down and says, "Was twenty minutes of magic enough for you boss?" McLean exploded. "You, get into that fucking dressing room and shut the door!"

'Archie Knox and I had a long relationship in the game, and of course we worked together for a period of years, but it didn't always go smoothly, particularly back in the early days. I was Clyde boss and we were at Station Park playing Forfar, where Archie was player-manager. Knox went up for a high ball with one of my guys, Sean Sweeney, and when they landed his studs twisted into Sean's ear. It looked really bad. I'm in the dugout, all smart with my Clyde blazer and shirt and tie on, and Billy McNeill, who's now in charge of Aberdeen and who I'd replaced, was there in the stand watching on. He says what unfolded was the funniest thing he's ever seen at a football match. The game is continuing, the referee hasn't seen what's happened, and I run on to the pitch and I'm chasing after Knox. Just as I get to him he turns round – now Archie's a hard guy, he could have planted me one – but he got such a shock seeing me that he ran away. The match is going on all around us and I'm chasing him across the centre circle with my blazer and tie on. I had just gone mental, I was a raving lunatic in those days. Jim Renton was the ref, and he called two policemen over to frogmarch me off the pitch. Naturally, I landed up in bother with the SFA and got a five-match ban and a hefty fine for those days, of £150.

'I can be a fiery character, Knox certainly is, but even the

13

calmest, most gentlemanly of guys can lose it when you see an injustice. We were playing Japan in the Kirin Cup, it was a soaking wet pitch, and one of the Japanese players hits Rab McKinnon with the worst tackle you've ever seen, it was a real leg-breaker. The Scotland doctor was the late Professor Stewart Hillis, and I'd rarely, if ever, seen him lose his temper. He's standing alongside me by the bench and when that happened, he's off, straight across the track and on to the pitch remonstrating with the Japanese and the referee, and making a beeline for Rab to treat him. In that moment, he had just lost it.

'Incidentally, Knox continued to cost me money later in my career. When we were with Scotland in Zagreb, I'd been nipping away at the officials from the dugout, and had been warned. Wee Billy Dodds got assaulted by the Croatian defender Igor Stimac, but mindful of what had gone before, I bit my tongue. Archie wasn't for holding back though and I hear this stream of abuse and swearing blasting out. The fourth official calls over the referee and fingers me. Now, I've never opened my mouth this time and I try to point out that I'm no ventriloquist, but I'm sent to the stand, and that's another ban and fine.

'A few months before the 1998 World Cup finals we played France in a friendly in St Etienne, and Ally McCoist isn't happy because he's on the bench and I'm playing Gordon Durie up front. McCoist, being the kind of character he is, is nipping away at me all the time, in a good-natured way, and I tell him to go and warm up, that I'll be putting him on to replace Gordon. Now, they're leading 1–0 at the time and as Ally's doing his stretching Durie equalises with a wonder goal, what a strike it was, he's smashed it into the top corner, and I realise there's no way I can take him off now. I call on McCoist and tell him to sit down in the dugout again, that I've changed my mind, and he points out on to the pitch, turns to me and says, "Durie? Durie? One goal in six years . . . Prolific, fucking prolific." I had to laugh, it was typical of Ally, but he never did get on that night.

14

'Many years later, when McCoist was the Rangers manager and I was in charge of Aberdeen, we were in the respective dugouts at Ibrox, and there was a challenge in stoppage time and it looked as if the referee was about to send off one of the home players. I didn't think that was necessary, so I wandered up to the fourth official to plead for clemency, and in the end only a yellow was shown. As I turn to walk back to the dugout, the Rangers fans in the enclosure are going crazy, and there's this one voice louder than all the rest, and the guy's screaming at me, "Hey Broon, ya bastard, trying to get him sent aff, ya wee bastard ya . . ." then he pauses, just for a moment, before delivering the follow-up, "and anyway, you're the only Scotland manager that ever got sacked fur shagging!" I burst out laughing, and McCoist hears this so he marches across from his dugout, lifts my arm into the air in the way you would with a boxer who'd just won a fight, and goes, "Yes!"

'That was just one of countless tales from the dugout down the years. It can be a humorous place, it can be an area of real anger and aggression. There can be confrontations that wouldn't take place anywhere else and there's undoubtedly irrational behaviour, even from the most unlikely sources.

'But the dugout is, and always will be, a hugely important part of football, a place from which games can be won and lost, and I've thoroughly enjoyed my decades down there.'

CHAPTER TWO

TALES FROM THE DUGOUT 1

JOHN McMASTER (ex-Morton coach)
We were playing Clydebank and they had a right good team at the time, gave us some real doings. That day the big striker Ken Eadie was running riot and they were 3–1 up at half-time. Allan McGraw gets the boys back into the dressing room and he's going through them, he's absolutely fuming, and he puts on three substitutes and sends them back out with a dire warning to improve in the second half. Within ten minutes it's 6–1 and I turn round and see our physio John Tierney absolutely gutting himself. McGraw spots him and says, "What the fuck are you laughing at?" and Tierney replies, "Substitutions worked well, didn't they?" Even Allan had to laugh at that one.

Another time, we're up north playing pre-season friendlies, three games in three days. We've been in Aberdeen and we've had a heavy night out and then on the Sunday we're playing Montrose. The dugouts at Links Park were like Second World War bunkers and they were split, so you had four of us in one bit and there was room for one or two in the other. One of our players gets injured on the far side and the ref stops the game and calls for treatment. Now I'm busy in my part of the dugout, I'm discussing with the manager who might go on if we need to make a change, and we suddenly realise there's no sign of

Tierney and the ref's still calling for the physio, he's whistling away and shouting across to us. So I pop my head round to see what's happening and big Tierney is lying there fast asleep, snoring his head off and with his feet dangling over the edge, dead to the world. So I shout on him and he suddenly wakes up with that 'where the hell am I' look on his face and just about smacked his head off the roof of the dugout.

DEREK FERGUSON (ex-Stranraer manager)

I'd taken over from Gerry Britton who'd got the Partick Thistle job, and I was enjoying the role, had a few decent players. One of them was James McKinstry, who played either full-back or wing-back, lovely fellow and did a good job for me, but this particular day he's started off terribly. Playing wide, he's right in front of me, so I'm trying to encourage him, and asking if he's okay, but he goes from bad to worse, keeps slicing the ball out of play or giving away possession. I ask the physio, I ask my assistant Colin Lindsay and the substitutes if he'd been fine beforehand, had anything happened, and I'm getting shakes of the head and blank looks.

We're not long into the game and I'm already thinking I might have to take him off, which I really didn't want to do as I'd have hated having that done to me as a player. I always liked a wee cup of tea early in the first half and so the coach driver, Stewart Marshall, comes down to the dugout and hands it to me. I ask Stewarty if James had been okay on the bus down, and he says, "Yes, but he's having a nightmare, you're going to have to get him off the park." Stewart's been driving the team around for forty-odd years, in fact his father had the job before him, and he's a huge Stranraer fan, so I say "right, if you really think that, you make the decision". He doesn't have to think twice; he immediately reaches down for the number board and that's it, the bus driver has decided – McKinstry got the hook after twenty minutes!

STUART McCALL (ex-Sheffield United assistant manager)

Neil Warnock was my boss, and he was such a wind-up merchant. We were at Anfield, playing Liverpool on the first day of the season, and he's out there at the edge of the dugout and he's shouting all sorts of nonsense, making sure Gerard Houllier and his coach, Phil Thompson, can hear every word. All he's doing is looking to get a reaction, and he does, because Thompson is quickly out of his seat going nuts, and screaming over towards us. Neil just smiles, sits back down, and says, "Right, that's them riled up, they've lost their focus on the game, you get out there and coach our lads." He was dead right, I looked round at Phil, and he's gone, completely, he's lost it totally, you can see it in his eyes.

Working under Warnock was quite an experience and I learned plenty from him. Given the amount of bans he incurred, I also spent quite a lot of time in charge of our dugout. To get round that, Neil decided we'd use a radio system to allow him to keep in touch with me from the stand, so before one game he hands me this earpiece and tells me to keep it switched on. I say fine, just give me a shout if you want to make a tactical change or a substitution, I'm thinking it'll be no real bother. The game kicks-off and Warnock immediately launches into what is effectively a radio commentary . . . "Stuart, Stuart! Their centre-half is coming out with the ball. Stuart, Stuart! Their full-back's just overlapped and sent in a dangerous cross. Stuart, Stuart . . .!" This is doing my head in, I'm thinking, 'I know gaffer, I can see what's happening' and eventually I rip the thing off and hand it to our fitness coach, Tony Daley, and tell him to listen in. After that, we just relied on the good old-fashioned shout from the stand – he was only sitting about eight rows back in any case!

BARRY WILSON (ex-Ross County)

I was about seventeen and just breaking into the Ross County first team and I was on the bench for a game we're playing down at

Fort William. It was a miserable day, rain and mist, and of course you're playing right under the shadow of Ben Nevis. It couldn't have been gloomier, but we were winning comfortably, and my Dad (Bobby) who was manager at the time decided to make a substitution, and take off our big centre-half, Johnston Bellshaw. You wouldn't normally take off your central defender unless he's injured, but Johnston was as blind as a bat, had forgotten his contact lenses that day, and the way he had been playing it looked like it. He was missing everything. He's normally a placid guy, but he was raging at being subbed, and he came storming off the pitch shouting and cursing, and straight into the home dugout. He's going crazy, he's firing off volleys of abuse, can't believe he's been taken off, and turns to Henrik Madej, the Fort manager, and tells him so in no uncertain manner, still unaware he's in the wrong dugout. Henrik turns to him and says, "Big man, I agree. You were my best player today, I'd have kept you out there." We're all in fits of laughter of course, and Johnston finally realises where he is and has to sheepishly walk across to join us.

WILLIE YOUNG (ex-referee)

For much of my career there was no such thing as a fourth official, but it became more prevalent later on and it was a role I took on many times, particularly on the international scene. I was down there between the dugouts for League Cup and Scottish Cup finals, and I did the UEFA Cup final in Moscow with Hugh Dallas between Parma and Marseille in 1999. The last match of my refereeing career was as fourth official at the 2005 Scottish Cup final between Dundee United and Celtic, and by then it was a position I had well and truly grown into and enjoyed doing. That was partly down to the experience I had amassed by then, but also because the job was a more satisfying and more important one.

At the start you were really only there in case the match referee

19

got injured, but over time you got the chance to be more directly involved in the game and to play a part in the decision-making process; you would look out for offences and be much more of a help to your colleague out in the middle. But your biggest job was always keeping a lid on things in the technical areas, and you had to be constantly vigilant, always ready for things to kick off.

More often than not it wasn't necessarily a major incident that sparked things – disallowed goals, penalty claims; of course they were contested – but a seemingly innocuous challenge in the centre circle, or a throw-in by the halfway line could also cause managers to spontaneously combust, depending on the score or their general mood at any given time.

As I got further on in my career and had built up relationships of sorts with most of the characters, I could use my sense of humour and my banter to defuse things, and that generally worked, but it took some time to reach that stage. When you're a young official just starting off, the guys, whether they be players, managers or coaches, don't acknowledge you as an individual. You're just 'the ref'. It was only when they started moaning and shouting at me using my name that I knew I was getting somewhere!

The one exception was with Celtic where every captain throughout my time refereeing would address me as 'Mr' which I think was a throwback to the Jock Stein days. I met Paul McStay recently at a golf event and he asked, "How are you Mr Young?" That made me laugh, and I replied, "Paul, you must be fifty years old by now. I think it's fine to call me Willie."

JIMMY NICHOLL (ex-Northern Ireland assistant manager)
It was November 1993 and the final game in qualifying for the next year's World Cup finals in the USA. We were out of it, couldn't get through, but our last fixture was at home to the Republic of Ireland at the old Windsor Park and they needed a point to qualify as their two rivals, Spain and Denmark, were playing each other. There had been talk of moving our game to

Old Trafford or Wembley, but in the end it went ahead in Belfast, and as you can imagine, it was a pretty tense occasion. It was also Billy Bingham's last game in charge after seventeen years, and beforehand he'd stoked things up by talking to the press about the 'mercenaries' in the Republic team, guys like Andy Townsend, John Aldridge and Ray Houghton who hadn't been born in Ireland, but were happy to play for them, to get their international caps.

Anyway, it was 0–0 until late in the match and they were getting more and more nervous. With about a quarter of an hour to go we scored, Jimmy Quinn making it 1–0 with a brilliant volley from twenty yards. I'm leaping about celebrating and their bench went crazy. Jack Charlton was still in charge and he and his assistant, Maurice Setters, were not happy with me, and a few words were exchanged in the heat of the moment.

So they're now chasing the game, trying to speed things up, and of course we're in no hurry. The ball ran off the field at the halfway line and towards me in the dugout. At the front of the technical area there was a curve and a wee ridge separating it from the pitch, so with Houghton rushing across and screaming for me to give him the ball, I kicked it towards him, but it hit the kerb and bounced straight back to me. As he goes mental I kick it again, and again it hits the ridge and comes back towards me. It was completely accidental, but that's not how they saw it and it erupts down there.

Charlton and Setters are calling me for everything, they're coming at me from all sides, and of course hearing their voices and those of some of the players, I'm at the wind-up giving it, "Oh is it England we're playing tonight? I could have sworn it was Ireland." They really didn't like that! Eventually it calms down, and Houghton finally gets the ball, and a few minutes later Alan McLoughlin scores an equaliser and that's enough for them to qualify for the finals because Spain beat Denmark 1–0 in their game.

21

We're walking back to the dressing room and I'm getting abuse from them all, they're in my face, they're all screaming and shouting at me. When we're back inside, Billy makes a speech to the players, thanks them and wishes them all the best, and says that the big disappointment was that at the end of his last game in charge, Jack Charlton had refused to shake his hand. He then goes up and repeats that to the press, saying he found it embarrassing and didn't know why Jack had been like that. Billy hadn't seen what had gone on, hadn't been aware of me noising them up, and when the reporters asked Charlton why he hadn't shaken hands, I'm told he cracked up and said I'd been winding him up throughout and that he just lost the plot.

To be fair, he later sent down a message that he wanted to see Billy and came down, apologised, and they did finally shake hands. What a night that was.

ALEX TOTTEN (ex-Alloa Athletic manager)
When I was a young manager at Alloa I still liked to wear a tracksuit in the dugout, and my assistant, Gregor Abel, and the physio, Fred Rae, also wore identical ones. We were like the Beverley Sisters! There was one match when things weren't going as well as we'd hoped and there was a torrent of abuse from our technical area, which the referee heard and took exception to. His problem was that he couldn't make out which one of us had delivered it. He came across and asked who'd shouted at him, and the three of us all pointed at each other with innocent looks on our faces. In the end he said, "Well, if there's any more of that one of you will be sent to the stand. I don't know which one, but one of you will be."

TERRY BUTCHER (ex-England)
I was on the bench at Italia 90 for our final group game against Egypt which we won 1–0 to qualify thanks to a Mark Wright header. The manager was of course the late, great Sir Bobby

Robson, and while he was a fantastic man in so many ways, he did on occasion have difficulty with players' names. With the match raging on and Bobby trying to think of ways to secure the victory, he partly turned towards the dugout and shouted over his shoulder, "Stevens, go and get yourself warmed-up!" So, Gary Stevens, who was then my Rangers clubmate, sprinted off down the track and spent the next five or six minutes stretching and twisting, getting himself all ready for action. He then ran back up to the dugout and said, "That's me all sorted gaffer. I'm ready." Bobby looked at him in surprise. "Ready for what?" To which Gary replied, "To go on as a sub." The manager just shook his head and said, "It's not you that's going on, it's Trevor."

And he then sent Trevor Steven out to warm up, leaving Gary to take his seat back with us again, and duly get slaughtered by all the guys. In the end, I don't think either of them got on, but we did go on and win the match. It had been even worse four years earlier in Mexico when as well as Gary and Trevor, there was another Gary Stevens, who was with Tottenham at the time. That was all too much for Bobby, there was constant confusion, and eventually the three of them all just answered to each of their names.

ALEX SMITH (ex-Stirling Albion manager)

Throughout my time in the game I've been so lucky to work with some fantastic people, and right back in my early days in charge of Stirling Albion I had the legendary Bob Shankly there. He was a director at the time, but a football man through and through, and he was a big help to me as well as being an unintentional comedian who could cut you down with his one-liners.

One night I'm out working with the players, been doing all my new coaching routines, the fancy stuff I've learned at Largs (at the SFA training courses) and I'm standing in the dugout when Bob, as was his custom, came wandering down. "Do you think that did them any good Alex?" I replied that we'd have to wait until Saturday to find out, to which he responded, "Ach, just run the bastards into the ground, that's all they understand."

Now, we had a player called Robert Duffin, who was a great guy, but who'd get so frustrated that he could never get the last word with Bob. Robert was out injured, he'd burst his shoulder in a game at Montrose the previous month, and part of his recovery was to stand with his arms outstretched, palms pressed against the wall of the physio's room, almost like a crucifixion pose. Bob hated anyone being injured, you had to have a plaster cast on before he'd believe you couldn't play, and as we walked back down the tunnel he looked in and saw Duffin doing his exercise. As he gave him the once over, Duffin thought he'd get in first and said, "Mr Shankly, I feel like Jesus Christ standing like this," to which Bob replied, "You might feel like Christ, you might even look like him for all I know, but the big difference is he was back amongst us in three days . . . It's six weeks and there's nae bloody sign of you." Everybody in the room dissolved into laughter apart from Robert, while Bob just shut the door and left him to it.

DEREK McINNES (ex-Rangers)

I was a substitute for what turned out to be my last game for Rangers. We were up at Pittodrie and winning comfortably against Aberdeen, it was midway through the second half and I was bursting for a pee. I was just about to tell the coaching staff that I was going to the toilet when the manager, Dick Advocaat, turned and told me to get ready to go on. I wasn't sure what to do – I knew I wouldn't make it through the rest of the game – but then I noticed there's a little alcove in the dugout there, so I sneak in behind and I'm standing in there doing a pee and Dick's shouting, "Derek, Derek . . . Hurry up, get out there!" He just had to wait until nature ran its course!

PAUL SHEERIN (ex-Southampton)

I never got to make a first team appearance at Southampton, but I did get on the bench one day and saw one of the funniest things I've encountered in the game. The manager at the time was Dave Merrington and he could be a pretty lively character down in the dugout. That afternoon he was getting carried away over some decision which he'd felt had gone against us and he went racing out towards the edge of the technical area shouting and cursing at anyone and everyone. Unfortunately, Dave wore false teeth, and as he was screaming and spluttering, they came flying out of his mouth and skidded across the ash track. He tried to pick them up without anyone noticing, and of course he couldn't make a big thing of cleaning them as that would have made it more obvious, so for the rest of the game he was chewing grit and spitting it out while refusing to admit what had happened. None of us mentioned it, but we were all sitting there on the bench trying desperately to hide the fact we were helpless with laughter.

TOMMY WRIGHT (ex-Ballymena United manager)

I was involved in a game against Lisburn Distillery in March 2008 which became infamous in the history of football in Northern Ireland. It was always likely to be a tight match, and it was an important one as we were both chasing a top-six finish ahead of the split, the league is set-up there just as it is in Scotland these days. We went 1–0 up, they pegged us back to 1–1 and then we had a player harshly sent off. Early in the second half we had another sent off – the referee was having a stinker – but with just nine men, we somehow took the lead again.

The Lisburn boss was Paul Kirk, and we had previous. There had been a game between us abandoned in the past over at their place because their floodlights weren't working, and he blamed me for putting pressure on the ref that day to stop the match. I hadn't, but he didn't believe that. Anyway, he's less than happy of course, 2–1 down to nine men, and he's giving it plenty from his dugout, and our fans are going mental because they believe the ref is against us. Our goalie, Paul Murphy, took a whack in the face from one of their players and we knock the ball out of play so he can get treatment. It turned out he had a broken jaw, it was a horrible injury, and they had to get an ambulance on to take him away.

After that had all settled down, and it took a long time, we had the problem of how to replace him. I'd used all my substitutes, so decided to put my striker, Kevin Kelbie, in goal for the rest of the game. At that point, it really got farcical, as the kit-man didn't have a spare goalie's jersey and Paul was still wearing his on the way to hospital, so Kevin had to keep goal with a bib over his shirt. The game restarts with them taking the throw-in and of course we're expecting the usual fair play, that the ball will be returned to us, but Kirk shouts to his players to keep it and they launch it into the box. We cleared that one, but now we're under constant pressure and it's getting more and more feisty on the pitch and in the stands. Our fans' mood wasn't helped when the fourth official put up the board showing nine minutes of stoppage time, and as fate would have it, they go and equalise right at the end of it.

I go to shake hands with Paul Kirk after the final whistle and I have a go at him over the throw-in, and he says, "What goes around comes around." He's talking about the floodlight incident, which I had nothing to do with, and it all kicks off between us. The dugouts are at the far side of the ground, so we're walking across the pitch towards the main stand and we're pointing and shouting at each other, the players are all arguing with each other, and unknown to us, because we were so focused on each other, all the fans are now congregated around the tunnel and they're going crazy. There was a chair thrown on to the pitch and then, out of nowhere, the real headline maker. The next day's papers had the slogan 'LEG OF LAMB SHAME' but it was actually a big bone one of the supporters had bought from the butcher's for his dog, he'd somehow smuggled it into the stadium, and as everything was kicking off he threw it on to the pitch! I think that brought everyone to their senses and it settled down pretty quickly and we all headed back to our dressing rooms, although I gather the referee, Mark Courtney, needed a police escort to get him safely off the pitch. Of course, that wasn't the end of it, and a few weeks later we were up in front of the Irish Football Association.

The match observer had claimed Kirk and I had been throwing punches, which we hadn't, and the FA refused to look at video footage we had which proved our story, they wouldn't let us use it. The committee sent us out of the room and then called us back in a bit later to hear our punishment. The room was absolutely packed as we sat down and the vice president, David Martin, announced that we'd both been found guilty, were to be banned for eight matches and had an exclusion order placed upon us; we weren't to be allowed within one mile of the stadium on match days. Paul Kirk stood up and shouted, "That's a fucking disgrace!" and I felt like doing the same, but our club solicitor grabbed my arm and told me to sit down. We appealed and in the end the ban was halved and the exclusion order lifted.

I met Martin a few years later and asked what they'd been thinking about and he explained that it was soon after Jose Mourinho had beaten a dressing room ban by being smuggled inside the Nou Camp in a hamper, and that had been the Irish FA's way of trying to stop us from doing the same. I just shook my head in disbelief. We didn't behave well that day, and it certainly got out of hand, but the furore afterwards was way over the top.

CRAIG PATERSON (ex-Hibernian)
I was in the dugout at Easter Road one afternoon, and our striker Ally McLeod, another of the substitutes, was warming up in

front of me when a chant rang out all around the stadium for him to be brought on. "Ally, Ally, Ally McLeod!" It got louder and louder as more supporters joined in, and if it had been me, I'd have been delighted, but Ally just immediately sat down, pulled off his boots and started shaking his head. I asked him what he was doing, and he said, "There's no chance of (Eddie) Turnbull putting me on now, is there? He's not going to bow to pressure from the fans, is he?" And he was right, he never did get on.

ALLAN PRESTON (ex-Livingston assistant manager)

We had a 12.15 kick-off against Celtic and the boss Davie Hay liked to start matches in the stand, and he'd call me to pass on instructions. Five minutes into the match the phone rang and I answered, expecting it to be Davie. It was my Mum, not realising I had an early game, and she was asking me to bring home some groceries after the match. I'm trying to watch the play and get her off the line, and I see I've got another call coming in, and this time it is Davie. He's going crazy because the line was engaged and he wants to make a tactical switch. When I finally spoke to him after the game I had to confess I'd been talking to my Mum, and to be fair he did have a laugh about it. Eventually.

BILLY STARK (ex-St Mirren)

I was first exposed to Alex Ferguson when I was eighteen and had a trial for St Mirren in a pre-season friendly at Selkirk. I had a poor first half, improved to no better than average in the second, but he obviously saw something and I signed for the club on the bus on the way back up the road. I was on the bench for about half that first season and I have to say there weren't many laughs in the dugout with him, it was more like volatility contained. He'd only been a manager for about a year and a half and he was very much learning the ropes, so I saw him in his embryonic stage, which was . . . interesting!

It was so intimidating at times, I remember one day walking along to the ground with my father and not wanting to go inside, I was really close to breaking point, he'd taken it right to the edge. I don't think 'fear' covers it. You'd come in at half-time and it didn't matter whether you were winning or not, someone was getting it; you just had to try to make sure it wasn't you by making sure you didn't catch his eye. We were playing Celtic in a League Cup tie at Love Street and they were awarded a free kick. I turned my back, and as I did they took it quickly, played the ball over my head, and I heard this explosion from the dugout from the manager. Typically, they go and score from it. I was subbed off in the second half and had to sit alongside him knowing I was in big trouble, but he never said a word. We all go into the dressing room afterwards and I'm sitting in the corner when he comes in, picks up a boot – which had the aluminum screw-in studs – and he throws it at my head. I didn't need the stitches that Beckham needed all those years later, but he caught me a beauty. That was how he worked, and you either had to cope with it, or you were no use to him. I should say, I never turned my back on the ball again for the rest of my career!

NEALE COOPER (ex-Aberdeen)
First game of the new season, 1981–82, we had been thrashed 4–1 by Dundee United at Tannadice, and Alex Ferguson was going crazy afterwards. He ordered that no one was to go out, we had to stay in every night until the next game, a League Cup tie against Berwick the following Wednesday. Now, I'm a young lad, and I like a Saturday night out, so off out I went with my mates. I woke up the next morning and I'm thinking 'Oh no, what have I done?' because Fergie had spies everywhere. Into training on the Monday morning, nothing said. Same again on the Tuesday, and I'm relaxed now, I've got away with it. Wednesday night he's about to do the team-talk and he says, "Cooper, come with me."

So he takes me into the boot room and he asks, "Were you at Boodles (nightclub) on Saturday night?" and I admit that yes, I was, but just for a shandy. "And were you at Champers [another nightclub, and one of Cooper's regular haunts] on Saturday night?"

"No boss" I say. He looks me in the eyes, tells me I've got one last chance, and asks again. I realise at that moment the game is up. "Oh yes boss, sorry I forgot, I was there too, just for a wee while."

There's a silence, then he says, "You'd better have the game of your life tonight."

Now I think I only got ten goals for Aberdeen in all my time there, but would you believe it, I scored the first one that night and before I know it I'm in front of the dugout moonwalking and dancing around in front of the boss. He could only smile.

STUART McCALL (ex-Motherwell manager)

I always try to stay calm down in the technical area, in fact I'm usually so intent on concentrating on the match, that I'm rarely aware of what's happening in the other dugout. You'll get one of your coaching staff going, "Did you hear what they just said?" and I say no, I'm usually completely oblivious to it all. It's the same with the fans to be honest, I'll have a bit of banter with the Celtic or Hearts supporters, Aberdeen can be fun given my Rangers background, but it's generally pretty good-natured stuff. I never had much bother with our fans either.

I remember Terry Butcher (former Motherwell manager) asking how I was getting on with the guys behind the home dugout at Fir Park, and at that point I'd had no troubles at all, but there was one incident a bit later which sticks with me. We'd had a young side out against Hibs and things weren't going well, and one of the supporters was giving the kids a really hard time, berating them throughout. I can understand the frustrations, but this guy went over the score, so I turned and pointed that out, asking him to support the team. We scored soon after and I turned round again, and while everyone else was up celebrating, he was just sitting there clapping politely.

Full-time whistle goes, we've won the match, and I can't resist looking back into the stand with a huge, satisfied grin on my face, and he doesn't even respond, he just blanks me and legs it.

WILLIE MILLER (ex-Aberdeen manager)

It was a midweek match at the old Broomfield, and you always dreaded that walk from the pavilion along to the dugout. Sure enough, every step I took I was getting abuse from the Airdrie fans, and it carried on right throughout the match. There were a few regulars there and the language was unbelievable. They just never let up, and it was hard to concentrate on the game at times as you heard this constant flow of swearing. Eventually, with just a few minutes left, my coach Drew Jarvie could take no more and he turned round and told them to "Shut the fuck up!" Next thing I know, there's a policeman in the dugout standing next to him and warning him about his improper language. They'd only gone and reported him!

MARK McGHEE (ex-Reading manager)

We were down at Exeter, October 1993, and we went on to win the Second Division title that season. We had a good team, and we were cruising, 4–1 up at half-time and I'm feeling calm and relaxed. Within a couple of minutes of the restart they've scored twice and I'm convinced both goals were miles – and I mean miles – offside. The dugouts at the time were below pitch level and I'm hanging out screaming abuse at the linesman, I'm talking serious illogical and completely ridiculous abuse. After the second one I jump out and I thought I was having an embolism, I was dizzy, my brain almost popped. My lot behind me are killing themselves laughing and the linesman, to his credit, never once reacted – I don't know how given what he was getting from

31

me. Anyway, we get another, I calm down again and we go on to win 6–4.

As I'm leaving the stadium I get handed the video of the game and we sit down to watch it on the team bus, and to my horror I see that both goals were well onside, the linesman was absolutely correct. The next morning I got his address from the club secretary and sent him a letter apologising profusely, and he wrote back thanking me saying he'd had that kind of abuse loads of times, but that I was the first person who'd actually contacted him to say sorry. That at least made me feel a little bit better.

BILLY BROWN (ex-Berwick Rangers assistant manager)

When Jim (Jefferies) and I took over at Berwick Rangers in 1988 we were even more excitable back then, and one afternoon at Montrose, after a particularly spectacular outburst when we disputed a throw-in, the referee Sandy Roy sent us to the stand. At the time, the front row of seats was right behind the dugout, so all we had to do was nip over the wee fence and stand there bawling and shouting as normal. We got hauled up for it of course and got a one-year touchline ban and were fined £300 each. My part-time take home wage at the time was £7.50 a week, and the club wouldn't pay the fine, so that was one costly throw-in. You'd think I'd have learned my lesson, but no. I still dispute throw-ins to this day!

DAVE BOWMAN (ex-Forfar)

I got involved in my fair share of incidents on the park and in and around the dugout, but I suppose the one most people remember was that game at Stranraer in September 2001 which landed me a seventeen-match suspension. The referee, Alan Gemmill, had sent off Robbie Horn with just a few minutes to go in a match we were clearly going to lose, and I asked him to reconsider, tried to have a joke with him, as it was a harsh decision. He wasn't having any of it, my language got more colourful, and he sent me off too. I refused to go, he asked me again and flashed the red card at me, and I knocked it out of his hand. By that point it was in for a penny, in for a pound. Eventually I left the pitch and I was absolutely raging.

Our manager, Neil Cooper, was standing in the dugout as I stormed past and I think he was about to say something to me, but saw the look in my eyes, saw I had gone completely, and just retreated to the bench, which was probably wise. I went inside, I booted the dressing room door, I booted another door, and the red cards just kept mounting up. I had been banned for seven games the previous season for amassing four reds in a match against Berwick Rangers, so I was hardly expecting leniency, but when I heard the following week it was a seventeen-game suspension it just convinced me the authorities had it in for me by then. I was going to chuck it – I was thirty-seven at that stage – but Maurice Malpas persuaded me not to let my career end like that, so I served it out and came back the following spring and played four more games for Forfar before hanging up my boots.

I was at Hampden recently and the ref came up and introduced himself to me, shook my hand, and said, "I'm the guy who sent you off that day." To be honest, I wasn't sure how to reply, what was I meant to say? It was a brief conversation.

BILLY DODDS (ex-Dundee United assistant manager)
We had just signed the Spanish striker David Fernandez from Celtic and we put him on the bench for a game against Hearts at Tannadice. We'd got off to a terrible start, they were 2–0 up early on, and 'Chis' (United manager Gordon Chisholm) was getting more and more frustrated in the dugout. We missed a good chance and he flipped. Before the game I'd been slaughtering him because he'd bought a new pair of shiny slip-on shoes, and as he lost it, he kicked out at a water bottle. He connected, but his new shoe came flying off and smashed David right in the face. Here's our new signing, hasn't even kicked a ball for the club,

and the manager's just split his chin open in the dugout. He had to go off with the doc and get three stitches at half-time. I really didn't know how to handle it. I'm standing there watching it all happen and suddenly our new striker is bent over in the dugout holding his face, blood streaming through his fingers.

I looked at 'Chis', then bent down to check David was all right. He was really funny about it afterwards. He was asked by reporters what had happened and he said, "I'm really scared of my new manager. I hadn't even been on the pitch and he does this to me . . . imagine what he'll do if I play badly for him!" 'Chis' had to admit it all, of course, and was quoted in the papers as saying, "It's not the best start to our working relationship." That has to be one of the biggest understatements of all time.

STEPHEN CRAIGAN (ex-Motherwell)

It was November 1996, I'm just a kid, and I've been included in the first-team match-day squad for the very first time. We were playing Hibernian at Easter Road, and although I wasn't really expecting to get on, I was quite nervous about the whole thing. I'm sitting on the bench and the first half hasn't gone that well, and at half-time we're 1–0 down and tempers are getting a bit frayed in the dressing room. Suddenly things kick off between the manager, Alex McLeish, and our centre-half, Brian Martin. They're screaming at each other, the insults are flying, and the guys are jumping in trying to haul them apart. As I got older I learned that's what we call 'passion' in the game, but as an inexperienced youngster I'm sitting there in fear, thinking, 'Please don't fight!'

I witnessed similar incidents throughout my career, I've seen teammates lay each other out cold with a single punch, there's been broken noses and blood everywhere, but I was never one for getting involved. I also learned very quickly when to keep my mouth shut, especially when your manager is in full flow.

After one defeat against Dundee at Dens in which we had

played particularly badly and lost a late goal, the gaffer, Terry Butcher, came storming into the dressing room. He was in full rant mode, everyone was getting it, but he clearly needed to find another way to fully express his emotions. He looked around the room, saw a water dispenser sitting in the corner, and gave it a full-blown kick. The plastic cups were scattered around everywhere and the unit disintegrated as water began to gush across the floor. Terry seemed oblivious and continued his tirade as we surreptitiously tried to lift our shoes and bags out of the way of the oncoming flood, while at the same time desperately trying to keep straight faces. Eventually he finished and stormed out, slamming the door behind him, while we all collapsed in fits of laughter and rescued our gear.

JIM JEFFERIES (ex-Hearts manager)

We had lost 1–0 to Rangers at Ibrox, a game the St Mirren manager Tom Hendrie had been at on a spying mission as his side were due to play the both of us soon after. He had commented later in the press about our tactics, about how defensive and negative we had been in our approach, and that niggled me. He was a young, inexperienced manager, but he should still have known better than to talk publicly about my team. It rebounded on him mind you, as they went there and lost 7–1. The following week we were at Love Street and when Colin Cameron put us ahead with a penalty, I'm shouting across to his dugout, "Our tactics okay today Tom? We doing okay?" I'm not proud of that, of winding him up, but he had really bugged me, and when we scored again, I did it again. It was just a way of sending a message to him, and the dugout was the perfect place to do it. And we got on fine together after that.

WILLIE MILLER (ex-Aberdeen captain)

We were playing a pre-season friendly against one of the Inverness Highland League sides, in fact we had two or three games on that day, so it was a select side up there and we were short of a physio. Alex Ferguson decided that his assistant, Archie Knox, could be physio for the day – it was just a friendly, nothing serious would happen . . . Just coming up to half-time I take a head knock, it doesn't seem anything major, so I just get up and get on with it. Very quickly though the blood is streaming down my face and into my eyes and I have to call for the game to be stopped. So, across from the dugout runs bold bag-man Archie who, as it turns out, can't stand the sight of blood. He takes one look at me, shouts, "Oh God. Oh my God!" and promptly runs off the pitch again screaming. Fergie now has to come on and I'm immediately sent up to Raigmore Hospital to get the cut stitched up. It doesn't quite live up to Archie's hard man reputation, does it? He was off the pitch like a scared wee boy that day!

PETER HOUSTON (ex-Falkirk)

When I was playing at Falkirk, Jim Duffy came and took over as manager, and there was a reserve match at Brockville one night. Now things were tight, we were a part-time club, and we didn't have a full-time physiotherapist. The guy who normally helped out couldn't make it that evening, so Duff decided he would be the physio for the night and he picks up the first aid bag and heads out of the dressing room. I'm standing in the dugout alongside him, keeping an eye on some of the younger players and offering a bit of help and advice. One of the guys goes down injured, and Jim suddenly remembers he's the physio, so he turns and quickly grabs the bag by his feet and runs on to the pitch. Our stricken player is lying there in pain, he's grabbing his calf and he's calling out, so Duff reaches him, bends down to get the sponge out and realises that what's he's actually picked up is one of the players' soap bags. Without missing a beat, he pulls out a can of hair gel, squirts some on to his hands and then starts rubbing it on to the player's head. The guy asks what the hell he's doing, and Jim replies, "I can't do anything for your fucking leg, but at least your hair's going to look good."

JIM DUFFY (ex-Falkirk manager)

It was John Gallacher who'd gone down, and to be fair I could see right away that it was cramp, you don't need to be a qualified physiotherapist to spot that. It was one of those big tubs of gel the boys used at the time that was in the bag, so I just got a lump of it and spiked up his hair. John was a bit confused at first, but he did have a laugh about it, and even though I say so myself, I did a good job with it, he looked great! And I got rid of his cramp.

NEIL SIMPSON (ex-Aberdeen)

One afternoon it was pouring with rain, the pitch was soaking, and perfect for slide-tackles. The ball bounced free just on the halfway line in front of the dugout and I heard Alex Ferguson shouting on me to get to it. I launched myself towards the ball and it must have been one of the best tackles of my career. I won it cleanly, but I couldn't stop and went sliding across the surface completely taking out the referee, Bob Valentine. He went somersaulting up into the air and landed on the pitch in a heap as I slid right over the touchline and into the technical area. He was fine, just a bit shaken, but that was a very satisfying moment and the crowd loved it. What a cheer I got for that one!

Back then, the Aberdeen players were well known for swarming around the referee to try to put pressure on him. It was a deliberate tactic, one of Alex Ferguson's orders, but the SFA obviously got wise to it and brought in a rule that any player charging towards the ref would immediately get booked. First game of the season the referee came into the dressing room beforehand and reminded us, said that he would have no option but to give us a yellow card if it happened. Five minutes gone, there was a bad tackle on Gordon Strachan and I instinctively sprinted towards the ref, but just as I reached him I remembered the directive, so I put on the brakes and in my poshest, politest voice asked, "Excuse me sir, I would like to enquire as to what action you might be considering taking in the wake of that robust challenge by my opponent?" Mark McGhee was nearby and he said, "What the fuck was that all about?" The ref just laughed, and I never got booked.

ALLAN PRESTON (ex-St Johnstone)

It was the final day of the season and we were finishing off at home to Dundee knowing a win would qualify us for the UEFA Cup. Paul Kane scored with a diving header pretty late on and we're all rushing around the pitch celebrating when I turn towards the dugout. The club doctor, Dr McCracken, was one of the nicest, quietest men I knew, but a real St Johnstone diehard, and he completely lost it. I see him rushing towards the pitch and sliding along the grass on his knees, fists clenched. It was incredible, unbelievable, but an example of how emotions become uncontrollable down there. If the ref had seen him he might have become the first ever club doctor to be sent to the stand.

JOHN McMASTER (ex-Morton coach)

Allan McGraw was the manager at the time, what a guy he was, and of course he's got the two walking sticks because of the injuries and the painkilling jabs he took as a player. We're at Raith Rovers and wee Gordon Dalziel is running riot, we're having a nightmare, and McGraw and his assistant Eddie Morrison aren't happy. Our midfielder John McNeil loses the ball and the gaffer goes crazy, he's sitting down with his stick in his hand and he goes to throw it down on the track, but it takes a bounce, and there's his stick spinning through the air until it lands on the pitch and near hits McNeil. Allan's a lovely man, but when he's angry he's one of those guys you just stay well clear of, so Eddie and I are sitting there trying not to laugh, our shoulders heaving, and McGraw is absolutely fuming. Next thing, the linesman's flagging and the referee comes over to see what's going on, and he can't believe it. Allan's trying to explain what's happened and the ref just shakes his head and hands him his cane back.

DEREK McINNES (Aberdeen manager)

You always have to be careful. I know the other managers will be reading and listening out for my quotes – I certainly read theirs – and so you have to make sure you don't give them anything they can feed off, anything they can use to motivate their players. I'm very careful, particularly post-match, to talk about my team and only very rarely about the opposition, because I don't want the other guy firing something at me from his dugout during the next match.

I do think the technical area might be a calmer place if we as managers got together more often, rather than just that head-to-head at three o'clock on a Saturday. If we had the chance to go away and just sit and talk about the demands and pressures of the job, I do think that would help to improve the respect. There would still be the bust-ups, but maybe it would be less personal. If we had those meetings a couple of times a season, it would be a chance to sit down, to have a chat away from the spotlight and to clear up any hangovers from previous games. In that kind of relaxed environment, we might get a better understanding of each other's problems and issues.

DEREK ADAMS (ex-Motherwell)

Season 1998–99 and John Boyle has taken over Motherwell, he's full of enthusiasm and ideas, and putting a bit of money into it. We're in Tenerife on the mid-season break, there for five days, did some training but not much, a couple of runs; it was more about having time to relax and build a collective team spirit, and we're going to be heading back to play Hearts twice in a row, once in the Scottish Cup at Fir Park then at Tynecastle in the league.

So John calls the squad together and he says, "If you beat Hearts in the Cup I'll give each of you a £3,000 bonus for winning the game, or you can take a chance; if you beat Hearts and then beat whoever you get in the next round, I'll give you £8,000, but if you lose in that round you get nothing." Now to be talking about that kind of money was ridiculous, it was incredible, so the boys get together and have a talk, and we decide to go for the gamble.

We beat Hearts 3–1, and then there's the wait for the draw for the fourth round, and we get Stirling Albion at home ... you can imagine the reaction to that. They had beaten Hibs in the previous round, but we won fairly comfortably by two goals to nil. You had to play in both games to get the £8,000 and I was substitute for the Albion game, you can just imagine how I felt in the dugout that day. I'm bouncing around desperate to get on the pitch ... never been so relieved as when Billy Davies turned to me and said I was going on with just about ten minutes left. I was buying a house at the time and that money came in very handy!

JOHN HEWITT (ex-Aberdeen)

The European Cup Winners Cup Final in Gothenburg, I'm a sub, and with two minutes left Eric Black gets injured and I go on to replace him. We see out the ninety, 1–1 against Real Madrid, and so it's on to extra time. We'd only been going a few minutes and I hear the manager (Alex Ferguson) shouting my name. I look across to the dugout and he's bawling, "John, you fucking stay up!" I'd come on, I was full of energy, and I was desperate to get involved, so I'd started dropping deeper and deeper to try to get on the ball, and he was going crazy. I got the message, pushed back up the field, and of course scored the winning goal, but he told me afterwards, once it had all died down, that if I hadn't followed his instructions he was going to sub me off again, which would have been quite a decision in a European final!

STUART KENNEDY (ex-Aberdeen)

I had been injured in the Cup Winners Cup semi-final in Belgium against Waterschei and I was obviously desperate to play in the final. I'd gone through a fitness test before we left for Gothenburg, and it had been agony, but Alex Ferguson had taken me aside and told me not to worry, he'd be putting me on the bench. It was an incredible decision as he knew I couldn't really take part in the match, and I respected him so much for that. Anyway, the game's raging on against Real Madrid, and he turns to me and tells me to go get warmed up. The rain is chucking down and I'm doing a few sprints, loosening off as I run up and down the track, doing some stretching, and the fans see me and they're singing and applauding me. After ten minutes or so I jog back to the dugout expecting to get the call and the manager tells John Hewitt to get changed, he's going on. I ask what's happening, why he'd sent me out, and he tells me I've had my bow in front of the supporters, my moment, and now to sit on my backside. It was another great piece of man-management, a compassionate act, so I settle back on to the bench, all the while telling him that had I got on I'd have scored two goals to settle the match. To be fair, John went and scored the winner, didn't he, so it wasn't such a bad substitution after all.

ALEX SMITH (ex-Aberdeen manager)

You have arguments with the other dugout all the time, quite often these people are among your best friends in the game, but that friendship is forgotten about during the ninety minutes. We were playing Rangers in November 1989, a Wednesday night at Pittodrie, and it had been a tough match. Graeme Souness and I were at each other constantly from our dugouts, and his mood wasn't helped when Hans Gillhaus scored a last-minute winner from David Robertson's cross. The move had started after we got a free kick, but the ball had rolled five yards forward and Jim Bett had taken it from there. Graeme had seen this and he was going crazy that the goal had been allowed to stand. Afterwards,

I'm in the long corridor under the main stand and I come face to face with Graeme. We nod, exchange a few words, and come to the first of a series of swing doors down there. He holds it open to let me through. By the time we get to the next one, there's not been much chat, but he's in front of me by now and has to hold the door for me again. This happens all the way down the length of the stand until we get to the doors nearest the dressing rooms and he's there first again. He turns to me and says, "You've just beaten me with a last-minute goal, from a free kick taken from the wrong place. If I have to open another fucking door for you I'm going to boot your arse the length of this corridor."

PETER HOUSTON (ex-Hearts assistant manager)
We'd been drawn against Braga in the UEFA Cup, September 2004, and we'd done really well in the first leg, beating them 3–1 at Murrayfield, although it was obviously still going to be a tough game in Portugal. The dugouts in their stadium were quite wide apart, maybe twenty or thirty yards, and when they scored first, early in the match, they're giving it plenty to our bench, gesturing to us. To be fair, we probably deserved that, because when Patrick Kisnorbo had scored our third goal in the final minute in the home leg, we'd gone absolutely mental and that was them responding. At the time I wasn't seeing it that way though, and I was raging, so when Mark de Vries equalised soon after, I was right across to their dugout celebrating in front of them. That wasn't such a good idea, they took it pretty badly, and I had to race back to our dugout with their entire coaching staff chasing after me. Big Craig (Levein) just looked at me, shook his head, and told me to get back on the bench and calm down, which I did, while the fourth official tried to hold off all the Portuguese.

ALEX TOTTEN (ex-Falkirk manager)
I always tended to get a bit overexcited in the technical area – I became a totally different person during the ninety minutes of

the match – and I had a habit of banging on the roof of the home dugout at the old Brockville when things weren't going my way. I did just that one afternoon, but hadn't realised that a young boy stood in behind had put his can of juice on the dugout. When I hammered on it, the can flipped up and poured its contents all over his head. The first I knew of it was when everyone else behind me started roaring with laughter.

Another afternoon we were down at Stranraer and the home fans were battering on the dugout and dangling their scarves over the front of it. The game wasn't going well, and they were getting to me, and eventually I snapped and grabbed a scarf and gave it a yank. Unfortunately it was round the neck of one of the supporters and I dragged him out on to the track. When a nearby policeman saw him there, he sprung into action ready to apprehend the intruder. He got quite a shock when he realised what had actually happened.

In my second spell as Falkirk boss I had Kevin McAllister as my assistant and the two of us were at the edge of the dugout shouting instructions. I'm getting more and more frustrated by the referee and I'm calling over, "Cassidy, you're hopeless! Cassidy, you're rubbish!" Eventually the ref wanders over and says, "My name's McGarry." McAllister just crumpled with laughter. I calmed down for a few minutes, but then there was another decision went against us and I shouted, "McGarry, you're worse than Cassidy!"

CHAPTER THREE

KENNY CLARK

Kenny Clark was a Class One referee for over seventeen years and presided over some of the biggest occasions in Scottish football during that time. From starting out in the senior game in January 1991, he reckons to have officiated at well over six hundred domestic matches until his retiral in May 2008. He took charge of the League Cup Final and Scottish Cup Final three times each, and after being promoted to the FIFA list was involved in more than one hundred international and European club ties.

As referee, as fourth official, and on occasion as assistant referee, he has amassed vast experience of the dugout, how tensions run out of control in the heat of the moment, and how best to defuse them. He has built relationships and understanding with many coaches and managers, realised when he needed to get right in the middle of confrontations and when he needed to take a step back, and developed and utilised his dry sense of humour which helped to calm even the most incensed of bosses.

Those populating the technical areas are well aware of what is expected of them down there, of what the boundaries are, and Clark says the job of the officials is to manage them sensibly, reacting to whatever kicks off rather than trying to lay down the law beforehand.

'There's very limited talking ahead of a match, because they've all got jobs to do at that time, so there's no point in getting too heavy about it all. What I've always felt important, from the moment you arrive at the ground, is building a rapport with everyone there, from the doorman onwards, letting them know you're actually a decent person and that you treat people the way you'd like to be treated. As for the players and managers, you have to realise they're all psyched-up on match-day, hugely so, and to expect them to exchange much small talk with you before the game would be stupid. Generally, the talk consists of superficial pleasantries and no more than that.

'There was a period, when Martin O'Neill was in charge of Celtic, that Stuart Dougal and Hugh Dallas stopped going into the Celtic dressing room to check the boots simply because they got the silent treatment. What they perhaps didn't realise was that we all got the silent treatment, but I decided I wasn't going to be cowed by that, I was deliberately going to go in and be chatty and lively, and see where we went from there. I got the silent treatment from some players, others would talk a bit, but obviously under duress, and I always reckoned that all came from Martin. He didn't talk to you before a match. If you were walking towards him in a corridor, he would go straight past with his head down and not take you on, and I suspect that was all about him just trying somehow to gain an edge.

'It was like that from my first encounter with him. I'd knocked on the door and gone in to check the boots, and the Celtic coach Tommy Burns stopped me, pointing out the manager was giving his team-talk. So I waited and waited, and eventually, as kick-off was approaching, decided to go round quietly trying not to disturb him. He broke off, and as I turned, suggested I might like to come in a bit earlier the next time. Now this was in front of the players, and he was obviously trying to make a point, so I replied that next time he should send someone to get me when he was free, and if I was ready, and it fitted in with my pre-match

45

preparations, I'd come along then. It was all a bit of jousting, like animals marking their territory I guess, but I would say that when it came to the dugout I had very little difficulty with Martin O'Neill, he was among the better behaved of the managers.

'I think we, as match officials, have to be very careful not to overstate our importance, both on the pitch and in the technical area. We have an important role to play, but have to ensure we don't overstep the mark, don't expect players or managers to kowtow to us before the game even kicks-off. Man-management is the most important function of a referee, showing respect and understanding, and that's as relevant between the dugouts as it is out on the field.

'That whole business of being nice to everyone around the ground has a part to play. If you make a mess of things in the first ten minutes, folk might just say, 'Ah well, at least he's a decent fellow' whereas if you've got everyone's backs up beforehand, they're desperate for you to fall flat on your face.

'When I was fulfilling the fourth official role you were right in the heat of it, and I became conscious early on that managers', coaches' and players' livelihoods are on the line and you can't expect them to conduct themselves like the local vicar. I always remember Jimmy Bone pointing out, "This is our workplace, so we use industrial language", and I understood that fully. I was also conscious, particularly in the bigger games, about the influence of the police and the Lord Advocate's guidelines and how important it was for us to try to stop the police having any cause to intervene. For example, the business of players being booked for going to the fans celebrating a goal, that has all come about from the police concerned about a crowd surge. I remember being at a security briefing one time, before it had become a mandatory caution, and a senior police officer, who had been match commander at Ibrox, telling me they wanted it brought in. I said, "Let me give you a scenario. It's 2–1 Rangers in an Old Firm game and John Hartson, who's already on a booking, scores with five minutes to go and runs to the Celtic support. You want me to send him off? Because there'd be a fucking crowd surge then!" He said "Point taken." People forget about that kind of pressure, what we're having to juggle with down there, but we can also use it to our advantage in calming down the managers.

'I remember being referee at Motherwell one day when the respective managers, Mark McGhee and Mixu Paatelainen, were at it all the way through the first half and the fourth official, Colin Brown, who was relatively inexperienced, had called me over to the dugouts a few times. They were definitely pushing it to see how far they could get with him. I waited until half-time then went to see the two of them individually and told each that the police had said that if either of them as much as farted in the second half they were getting lifted. Now the police hadn't spoken to me, but they didn't know that, the message got home, and the pair of them were as meek as could be in the second half.

'Sometimes you just have to be a little cute to control the technical area and those in it, on other occasions you use humour, and at times you have to be very firm with them, be prepared to stand toe-to-toe. Interestingly, I very rarely if ever had any problems when I was fourth official in European ties. Those guys were very frightened of UEFA, they knew they would be jumped all over and find themselves banned, so they were always very careful, more respectful generally than in games at home. To be honest, in some European games as fourth official you were all but redundant apart from holding up your board a few times, whereas in Scotland you were always first line of attack, and you knew that. You could have done with a suit of armour and a pair of earmuffs!

'I had running battles with many managers over the years, a lot of fun with them too, and chief among them was Jim Jefferies. For instance, he was the only manager who would personally deliver the team-lines to our dressing-room. At all the other clubs it would be the assistant, or a coach, but Jim did it himself and it was solely so that he could mark your card about some perceived injustice perpetrated on his team in an earlier game. It became a standing joke among referees. When we were having our pre-match lunch ahead of one of his games, we'd be asking, 'Right, what have you done to upset Jefferies lately?' You get to the ground, and sure enough he'd be in reminding us about an incorrect offside, or a goal chalked off, and he'd say, "That's one you're owe us."

'He came in one day (when he was managing at Kilmarnock), and asked if I was fourth official, and when I said yes, he said, "Good, I like you as fourth", to which I replied, "Aye, better than you like me as ref?" We had a laugh, and he made the point that he actually liked me there as he felt he could talk to me in a way he couldn't with some of the other guys. The game kicks-off and he starts, "Hey you, you bastard! What about that?" He kept this going throughout the first half, and I knew it was all a bit of fun and we were laughing about it, but I eventually had to tell him to stop as I could see we were getting funny looks from the Dundee United dugout, the guys there clearly wondering what the hell was going on.

'It had been a really drab game and about five minutes before half-time I get my notebook out and start writing in it. He asks what I'm doing and I tell him I'm keeping note of the score. "The score?" he asks, "It's fucking nil-nil!" I reply, "No, you're winning 3–2. I'm keeping score of the managerial clichés shouted from the dugouts, all that pish you're spouting." He asks, "You just think this is a laugh, don't you?" and I say, "Well, I've got to do something to keep me entertained. This is murder!"

'After the break, I'm standing on the touchline and I really am making a note of something, must have been a substitution I suppose, and he comes down that wee tunnel at Kilmarnock and as he passes behind me he thumps into my back and I stumble forward. I turn round, and he just gives me a wee smile. The folk in the stand must have wondered what on earth was going on, but it was all good fun, and that's the sort of thing that helps you when you need to try to instill order down there.

'One of the methods I used, both on the pitch and by the dugouts, was to call players and managers by their first names most of the time, but if they started to step out of line it would be Mr Lennon or Mr Jefferies, then 'Hey you!' and with the players if they really began to push it, it would be number four or number ten, whatever, and subliminally I think that had an impact, it just let them know where they stood and how close they were to action being taken.

'The further I went into my career, the easier I found it to handle situations. It was a combination of things I guess; you'd built up a rapport with the guys over the years and you were also more confident within yourself, more relaxed. You also weren't quite as worried about the guy (the referee observer) in the stand. Without being blasé about it, I knew in my last four or five seasons that unless I allowed someone to be beheaded in the dugout I wasn't really going to get much grief from the observer, it was just about keeping a lid on things.

'Experience helps enormously. I remember the late, great Tom Wharton saying to me years ago, "Relax and show your personality a wee bit, it's not a crime to smile on a football park." Early in my career I tried to be too strong and stern, but as I got more experienced, I realised Tom was absolutely right.

'Whether you're referee, running the line or fourth official, you're talking all the time, you're thinking all the time, and it's all about managing the game, about becoming aware of potential flashpoints and trying to defuse them. That's what separates the men from the boys. Anyone who gets to Class One knows what's a red card, knows what a foul is, but it's about how you sell your decisions to players and managers and how you keep them all on as even a keel as possible. For instance, every time I sent off a player I would be poring over that all night. Not about whether the decision was correct necessarily, but whether there was anything I could have done to try to stop that player from reaching that level of loss of control, what had I missed to allow him to get so frenzied?

'I tried to take the same approach to the dugouts, but it wasn't always as easy as that. Some managers simply didn't want the fourth official talking to them at all so that meant you couldn't do your job properly and you had to use strength of personality. You had to impress upon them that you had a job to do and let them decide whether they got the 'good cop' or 'bad cop' routine.

'Everyone talks about referees having, or not having, a feel for the game, and it's very similar when you're between the two dugouts; there you also have to have a feel for the mood and it's all about judging the moment correctly, whether it makes sense to take a step back or whether you need to confront the individual concerned.

'I would only ever call the referee over as a last resort, I would try to deal with things myself, and I still think the fourth official should have the power to dismiss a manager rather than having to get the ref involved. The last thing he needs in the middle of a heated, controversial game is to have to come across to the dugout and have a confrontation on the touchline. Given that the fourth official will always be a Class One, or indeed a FIFA referee in European games, I do not understand why he isn't allowed just to handle it himself. Being in that job is like being a guard dog with no teeth, there's only so many times you can say, "Any more of that and I'll call the referee across." I tried to be careful not to do that. If I said it, they knew I meant it.

'You obviously get to know the guys, get to know who you're going to have bother with. Take Gordon Strachan, he was great when he was at Celtic, I never had any trouble with him, but his assistant, Garry Pendrey, was a real pest. Gordon said to me one day just to leave Garry alone, and I told him I couldn't, that he was behaving like an idiot. Strachan asked what he'd said, I told him, and he said, "Fair enough, you carry on, give it to him with both barrels."

'I did have one very funny moment with Gordon when he was Coventry manager and they were playing Hearts in a pre-season friendly. Ian Frickleton was running the line and he gave an offside against Darren Huckerby. Huckerby started going crazy, and then Gordon came out and started chipping away too, so I went over and pointed out it was just a bounce game, that there was no need to be getting so animated, and the whole time I'm talking he's going, "I know, I know. You're quite right, absolutely, no problem . . ." agreeing with everything I said. So I turn to walk away and all I hear is, "Fucking awful decision though, wasn't it?" He's lulled me along, and then he's gone 'bang'. I mean, what can you do about that? I just had to laugh and get on with the game.

'Some of the most difficult occasions were when you were standing at the side of the pitch and you knew the referee was having a howler. That made it really tricky as to what you're meant to do, what you're meant to say to the managers and coaches who can see just as clearly as you can what's going on out there. You can't slag the ref off, because you know only too well that at the first opportunity the manager is going to call out to him, 'Even your mate thinks you're having a shocker!' The former ref, Brian McGinlay, fell foul of that years ago. Bob Valentine had been chosen to go to the European Championship finals and Brian and someone else were to be his linesmen; they were going out as a team, so the SFA gave them a few games in Scotland beforehand so that they could work together. Bob was having a particularly unhappy afternoon doing an Ayr United game at Somerset Park and as they came out for the second half the Ayr manager Ally MacLeod turned to McGinlay and asked what he thought. Brian, trying to be careful, replied, "Well, he's maybe not having the best of days . . ." at which point Ally turned to the whole main stand and shouted up, "Even he says the referee's fucking murder!"

'You obviously can't defend the indefensible, but you do try to put the referee's case across to the managers and coaches, pointing out the guy only gets one look at it, that he's maybe seen it from a different angle to us in the dugout, that he's called it as best he could at that split second. I remember Bobby Williamson when he was Kilmarnock manager saying to me that while on the one hand he didn't like fourth officials being there because they reined managers in, he did actually appreciate having them on hand because it helped to give him a far better insight into what the referee was doing and why he'd made certain decisions.

'The introduction of the fourth official has, over the years, eased the pressure on the referee and linesmen to a certain extent. The unwritten rule is that the dugouts are his domain, and you only get involved if you really have to. Of course, I had many games as assistant before the introduction of the fourth official and those could be particularly difficult as you were getting harangued by the crowd and the coaching staff for your mistakes as well as all the referee's.

'It did help if you had a strong, experienced referee out there and I remember early in my career running the line at Stenhousemuir one day. The ref was a lovely big guy, Mick McGinley from Clydebank, and he was a real mentor to me. I was heading down towards the corner flag and I could hear the Stenny manager, Terry Christie, who of course had his trademark duffel coat on, giving me absolute dog's abuse, calling me for everything. Big Mick sauntered over, had a word with Terry who slunk back into the dugout, and walked off, and I never heard another word from him throughout the rest of the match. When I asked Mick afterwards what he'd said to him, he replied, "I pointed oot tae him that where I come fae, grown men don't dance about wearing duffel coats."

'That was a great example of how to kill a situation dead. You don't need any great wisdom, you don't necessarily have to appeal to their better nature, or be particularly clever, but if you can assess the mood and find the right words, you can knock them off their stride and calm things down just like that.

'I was fourth official at one Old Firm encounter at Celtic Park, the game was in the melting pot, and two players, one from each side, went down injured at the same time, but separately. Stuart Dougal was referee and he stopped play for the Rangers player and called the physio on. He hadn't actually noticed the Celtic player was down too, that was happening behind him, and without him seeing, the Celtic physio had come on, treated his man, and trotted back off. He then ushers the Rangers player off the park as he has to after treatment has been administered, and I try to contact him to advise him what's happened, but my microphone system isn't working. The Rangers manager Walter Smith is going nuts, seeing his team a man down, and I try to explain to him that Stuart hasn't seen the Celtic physio coming on. "Well, you fucking tell him, that's what that thing's for!" is his response. I say, "Can I tell you something?" "What?" And I lean over and say, "It's fucked." And he just turns on his heels and walks back to the dugout killing himself laughing, much to the confusion of everyone else there. Just as I was congratulating myself on how I'd handled the situation I suddenly thought, 'Shit, there might have been a camera on me there' and you wouldn't have had to be a master lip-reader to work out what I'd said. Fortunately I got away with it and it certainly took the sting out of things.

'One of my favourite stories centres on the assistant Charlie Smith who was running the line at Cappielow for a young, inexperienced ref who was having a hard time of it and getting a lot of stick from the Morton dugout. Charlie turned to the manager, Jim McInally, and said, "Give him a break, the boy's only just started masturbating." One of the coaching staff actually went up to him and asked, "What did you just say?" They couldn't believe it, but they all started laughing, and again it was enough to defuse the situation and calm it all down.

'There are times when you just turn a deaf ear to abuse, you have to accept there will be swearing down there. If the guys use swear words to emphasise a point, like 'a fucking foul' I was never bothered by that, but if they aimed the swearing directly at me, or called me a cheat, then I took action. One night at East End Park when Dick Advocaat was Rangers manager, he was pushing it and pushing it. I was fourth official and Willie Young was referee, and eventually I warned Dick that unless he calmed down I'd call Willie over. He turned round dismissively and shouted, "He's a Celtic supporter and you are too!" Away he went.

'There was another game at Ibrox, again Willie was the ref, and Advocaat was out screaming and shouting at him. When he returned to the dugout I leant over and pointed out that Willie hadn't paid the slightest bit of attention to him, wouldn't even have heard him from that distance. He looked at me and said, "Yes, I know that, but the crowd expect that of me." It was all for show, all to let the Rangers supporters see how much he cared. We, as officials, have to be able to make the distinction between the dramatics for the sake of it and an actual loss of control or attempt to undermine our authority.

'There were many amusing and humorous moments, but one that always sticks with me was with Ebbe Skovdahl when he was Aberdeen manager. I was fourth official at Pittodrie and they were being well beaten by Motherwell, they'd been terrible that day. Ebbe turns to me and says, "I want to make a substitution." I remind him that I need the sheet of paper with the numbers of the players going on and coming off so that I can input them into my electronic board. He goes back into the dugout, then returns with the sheet but it's only got the number of the player he wants to put on. I tell him I need to know who he wants subbed off and he replies, "You pick. They're all pish." It doesn't happen often, but that one really knocked me off my feet and I eventually pointed out that it wasn't really in my remit to decide upon substitutions! In the end I got the kit-man, Jim Warrender, to choose which of them should get the hook.

'I have to be honest, I would always far rather be the referee out on the park than doing the fourth official's job because, more often than not, it seemed like a thankless task; you were getting all of the pain and none of the glory. That said, what I did like was that you were part of that inner cabal and you see things that other people wouldn't get the chance to see. I loved the humour you got in the technical area, but I also loved the insight and the awareness you developed of all the different personalities, the chemistry and the conflicts between people, all of that. I find the psychology of sport really fascinating and there's no doubt that you get that in microcosm when you're between the dugouts. It can be really tough at times, but I amassed some great memories, amazing experiences, and I'm glad I got the chance to do that over my years down there.'

CHAPTER FOUR

TALES FROM THE DUGOUT 2

ALEX SMITH (ex-Stirling Albion manager)
We were playing Queen's Park at Hampden and I was watching from the stand. Things weren't going well, and I was getting angrier and angrier, so I decided I had to make a change. I ran down the stairs and out along that tunnel, turned, and jumped into the dugout shouting, "Get Willie Irvine off, get him off!" I found myself face-to-face with the Queen's Park coach, Eddie Hunter, who was quite a character, and didn't take kindly to me having got into the wrong one. "Get the fuck out of my dugout!" was all he said. So I jumped back on to the track and ran along to our own one to make the substitution and I hear a couple of Albion fans from just behind calling out, "Aye, and you can get the fuck out of that one as well Smith!"

JIMMY CALDERWOOD (ex-Dunfermline manager)
It was one afternoon at Pittodrie and Aberdeen were giving us a doing. They were 2–0 up early on and I knew I had to make changes. To be honest, I could have taken any of the boys off, but I decided to substitute Jack de Gier and Ian Ferguson. 'Fergie' was absolutely furious as he stormed across to the dugout, which I could understand as nobody likes to be hooked just twenty-five minutes into the game. He gave me a blast, went crazy, and I told

him he'd been hopeless, that I had to take him off. "Why couldn't you wait until half-time? You know they fucking hate me up here!" The Aberdeen fans had been loving it right enough with his Rangers background and the rivalry between the two clubs, but there was no way I could have shown him any sympathy that day; it was a call I had to make.

The argument continued in the coach on the way back down the road and in the end I told him he was fined £300, which didn't go down well. On the Monday morning I'm sitting at my desk and I hear a loud banging on the door. Without even waiting for it to open, I call, "Yes Ian, how can I help you?" and he storms in and throws the money down on the table. "There's your three hundred quid."

When we had a team meeting later I waved the £300 in the air and said, "The first round in Magaluf at the end of the season is on Fergie." That at least got a few laughs and when we spoke about it after, and I pointed out that as he moved into football management he'd find himself in the position I'd been in, and would have to make the same decisions I did, he accepted it and it all settled down.

DEREK McINNES (Aberdeen manager)

Walter Smith always advised me to show respect to the opposing manager. Even if you don't like him, even if he's been an arse in his dugout during the match, go in and have a drink afterwards, or make sure you invite him to your office. That's always stuck with me, even if it is difficult in certain situations, but I do try to show that respect in the technical area because we're all in the same job, experiencing the same pressures, the same demands. Strangely enough, it can sometimes be the opposition staff that get a wee bit above themselves, so I always try to keep my staff in check, and that's not always easy when you've got Tony Docherty standing alongside you!

I always tell them I don't want us getting the reputation of being a dugout that's always up in arms over every decision, I don't want the physio, the goalkeeping coach and the kit-man all out there screaming at the referee. It becomes a bit of a rabble if that happens, looks a bit out of control. In any case, Tony and I do enough appealing – we don't need anyone else. You do try to show that respect, particularly if, as is often the case, there's a friend in the opposite technical area. It's not nice seeing a fellow manager standing there, clearly under pressure, because you know just what he's going through.

I remember when I was at St Johnstone and we beat Hibs 2–0 and big 'Yogi' (John Hughes) got sacked after it. I really like big John – I don't know if he knew it was coming, but standing looking across from my technical area I could see he was really feeling it that day. Hibs are his club, he was determined to do well, but we beat them and that led to him losing his job. Days like that aren't easy.

ALASDAIR ROSS (assistant referee)

I was refereeing a Rangers under 14s game back in 2001 and had a run-in with the club's coach, Jan Derks. One of their players had lost possession cheaply and went down with a 'phantom' injury to try to cover up his mistake. Derks started screaming from the touchline for the game to be halted, but I knew there was no need. Rangers then regained possession and Derks went quiet, only to erupt once more when his team got the ball back. Eventually he came on to 'treat' the player and all he would say to me was, "Fuck off referee, fuck off!" He went back to the touchline and continued to shout "Fuck off!" so I had to go over and send him away from the dugout. It was just a public pitch, there were no complaints from the rest of the coaching staff, and he proceeded to watch the rest of the game from the car park. Afterwards he came in to apologise, said he couldn't believe he'd behaved that way, it had been shocking, and he was sorry. He assumed we could shake hands and that would be the end of it. As soon as I pointed out that because I'd had to take action against him, I now had to write a report and submit it to the Scottish FA, I had no choice, he said, "Fuck off referee," and walked out. All this had to be written verbatim in my report. Rangers, knowing he didn't have a leg to stand on, sent no one to represent him at his hearing, and he got a three-month ban from all football activities, and was sacked soon after.

ALLAN PRESTON (ex-St Johnstone)

We were playing our big local rivals Dundee on New Year's Day 1997 and we were thrashing them, 7–1 up with just a few minutes to go and we were absolutely buzzing. They got a late second goal, but we weren't bothered. We weren't, but the assistant manager John Blackley was. I was playing on the dugout side and I hear him shouting and screaming, so I turn round just in time to see his false teeth flying out of his mouth and skidding across the red blaise track. He shoved them back into his mouth and at the end was giving us stick for losing the late goal, but they're falling back out and there's grit dribbling down his chin, and we're in fits of laughter. He just had to give up.

CALLUM DAVIDSON (ex-St Johnstone)

I'll never forget that day, it was so funny! I was on the bench and it was Danny Griffin who gave away the penalty from which Dundee got that late goal. John went absolutely mental, he flew out of the dugout in such a rage and then he just stopped, just went quiet. He had his back to us, so we had no idea what had happened. And then we see him bending down to pick them up and he's trying to clean them, to get all the dirt off them. The whole bench just collapsed and it's one of those stories that comes back every time the lads get together. It was such a brilliant moment.

TERRY BUTCHER (ex-Dundee United coach)

Maurice Malpas and I were in charge of the side for an under-21 game at Fir Park against Motherwell, and John Blackley, who was assistant manager to the boss, Paul Sturrock, decided to come along as he wanted to watch some of the younger players in action, with a view to maybe getting them into the first team squad. There was an incident happened out on the pitch, nothing major, but it angered John and he went ballistic. He'd been in at the corner of the dugout, and was in such a hurry to get out to the side of the pitch that rather than go past everyone else, he tried to leap over the little wall so that he could berate the ref as quickly as possible. Unfortunately, he stumbled, fell face down on the track, and his false teeth went flying across the ground. He scrambled around, grabbed them, and shoved them back in his mouth, shouted at the referee, then turned back towards us. The dirt was dribbling down his chin and his face was filthy, but none of us said a thing. We just stood there, didn't flinch, and pretended we'd been watching the game all along as if nothing had happened.

Those teeth of his did cause him problems. I've seen him giving a team an absolute rollicking for ten minutes full-on in the dressing room, and the faster he spoke, the louder he got, the more his falsies wobbled around in his mouth. I've seen spit dribbling down his face as he ranted in full flow, but he was such an intimidating character that not one single player ever dared even to crack a smile. He's a lovely guy, a brilliant coach – I learned so much from him – and he was a superb player, part of that fantastic Hibs team of the 1970s, but his personal habits could be a bit much. The room the coaches used at Tannadice had three baths in it, and quite often we'd be in there eating our lunch and John would be having a soak and cutting his toenails and they'd be flying everywhere!

STUART McCALL (ex-Rangers manager)

My time as Rangers boss ended in huge disappointment, and in farcical scenes, with the play-off defeat against Motherwell back at my old home, Fir Park. They'd beaten us comfortably and it had been torture standing in the dugout watching the game being played out, so as soon as the final whistle went I shook hands with Ian Baraclough and the rest of the Motherwell coaching staff, made a sharp exit from the technical area, and headed straight up the tunnel. I couldn't have been more than twenty feet down it when I heard uproar behind me, so I turned and ran back out on to the pitch to see an all-out battle taking place. I dived in, still unaware of what had gone on, and helped try to pull the players apart. I learned later of course that Lee Erwin had given Bilel Mohsni a wee push and that Mohsni had responded by kicking him on the backside and then landing a punch flush on his jaw, which had led to the melee that followed.

Once it had all calmed down and I was heading off again, one Motherwell fan leant over and gave me a volley of abuse, the politest part of which was the suggestion that I was 'a fucking wanker!' I asked why, he backtracked a bit and said that I wasn't, that it was actually Mohsni who was, and I suggested he tell the player that, not me. In the end, he actually went, "Sorry Stuart, no offence," which was another bizarre little cameo in an incredible afternoon. I went to do the press afterwards, was naturally asked about it, and told the reporters that I hadn't seen what had happened, which was the truth.

When I went home I wanted to have a look for myself – I've never watched back any of the game itself, and never will, but I felt I had to see that – and as I'm watching the footage I'm thinking, 'who's that wee ginger-haired guy running around right in the middle of it all?' It just goes to show how easily things can be distorted. I genuinely had no idea what had gone on and was just trying to act as peacemaker, but for anyone looking on it must have seemed as if I was one of the main protagonists.

DEREK FERGUSON (ex-Rangers)
We were playing Steaua Bucharest in the quarter-finals of the European Cup, March 1988, and they had some team, real stars

like Hagi and Lacatus. I always remember Ally McCoist had been in for a cartilage operation just a few weeks before, but the manager was desperate to play him, and he was passed fit to start. I was on the bench, and when we came out the old stadium was absolutely packed, but as you looked around you could see it seemed mainly to be soldiers, it was as if they'd drafted the army in to fill the seats. The other thing that struck me was that it was eerily quiet, there was hardly a sound to be heard. That changed as soon as the game kicked off, and it got even louder when they scored after just two minutes. I remember turning to the other subs and remarking on the atmosphere, just how good it was, incredibly noisy. It went on and on, never let up, so I started glancing round from the dugout to see what was happening and all I could see were people sitting blank-faced, not at all animated, it was so strange. I couldn't understand what was happening until someone pointed out some big speakers placed around the pitch – they were piping in fake crowd noises over the PA system to generate the atmosphere and it continued right the way through the match. I never yet saw one fan shout or celebrate, but that was one of the loudest stadiums I ever played in!

LEE MAIR (ex-Aberdeen)

It was a game against Hearts late in 2008 and I'd been on the bench. We were 1–0 up, they'd had Zaliukas sent off, and things were getting a bit heated. I'm warming up and I get the shout from Jimmy Calderwood in the technical area with just a few minutes to go. I get stripped quickly and I'm standing at the edge of the dugout getting my instructions, we're going to be tightening things up at the back, making sure we don't let in a late equaliser. We see it through and as the final whistle goes I'm aware of our young striker Chris Maguire getting involved with Robbie Neilson. It was handbags really, but it carried on as the pair of them went up the tunnel, so the rest of us make a beeline for it. Before you know it, it was a mass brawl up there. The tea lady's standing back, there are staff around the edges, and there are thirty-odd players and coaches all going at it. I grabbed Robbie and he turned and punched me and it kicked off even further. Honestly, it was like 'Royal Rumble', everyone running down the tunnel and just piling in. It got to the point where I was standing just swinging haymakers, hoping they would land on someone in a Hearts strip rather than on one of my own team-mates. It was self-preservation; if you were swinging punches, you were less likely to get hit yourself.

Wee Chris started it all, and he's now hiding in a corner. Suddenly the shout went out, "Here's Nadé!" and at that point we bolted for the dressing room; no one was going to take on big Christian Nadé, who was just a beast. I heard later it took them half an hour to calm him down, that he was set on charging into our room and taking us all on. I've seen a few bust-ups in my day, but that was the biggest by far.

PAUL SHEERIN (ex-Arbroath manager)

We'd been promoted as Third Division champions in 2011 and were going for back-to-back promotions the next year, finishing runners-up in the Second Division to make the play-offs. We were up against Dumbarton, who'd finished in third, and we'd lost the first leg narrowly at their place. Stuart Malcolm had put us in front, but although they'd come from behind to win 2–1 we still had a real chance in the next game at Gayfield. It was a tight one, still 0–0 late on, and I was getting more and more excited in the dugout.

It was a big afternoon for the club of course, we had a big crowd in, and all my family were in the main stand behind me. In the heat of the moment, I'd forgotten all about that, and with us pushing to try to get that goal, I'm leaping about all over the place, frustration kicking in. I know it's just about the end of the ninety minutes, so I'm looking across at the fourth official to see how much stoppage time there's going to be. There had been four or five substitutions, and the physios had been on a couple of times, so I'm hoping for plenty, and when I see the board with the number three going up, I explode, "Three minutes? You've got to be fucking joking! Three fucking minutes?" I'm ranting and raving, I can't believe it, and of course the three minutes pass without us scoring, and that's it, we're out.

It was really disappointing, such an anticlimax at the end of what had been a brilliant season, and eventually we got away from the ground and home to relax with a few glasses of wine. I was sitting in my chair just reflecting on the afternoon when my five-year-old daughter, Dervla, suddenly jumped up and did an impersonation of me in the dugout from earlier, quoting me word for word! It was only at that point that the realisation sunk in just how fraught things can get down there, and how you really have to be careful about how you act and what you say.

WILLIE YOUNG (ex-referee)
Sandy Clark was one of the game's biggest moaners, and he always liked to make sure he got a chat after matches to get a particular point across. When he was Hamilton manager I was doing a game between them and Morton at Cappielow and correctly awarded the home side a penalty from which they scored the winning goal. I was sitting in the changing room afterwards and there was a chap on the door. I turned to my assistants and said, "That'll be Sandy," and sure enough in he comes. He was pleasant enough: "Well done Willie, you had a good game . . ." but as he was leaving, he turned and said, "But what about that fucking penalty, it was a bit soft, eh?" I looked over to him and replied, "Sandy, I've been doing this job for about fifteen years now, and I've learned that penalties are like boiled eggs. You can get soft ones and you can get hard ones, but they're still a boiled egg." He just looked at me, shook his head, and walked out.

Jim Jefferies was another who liked a moan and it would be

fair to say we had something of a fraught 'love-hate' relationship at times. He would fume at me, I would fume at him, but we pretty much just got on with it. He gave me more trouble earlier in my career, but that changed all of a sudden, and I only found out why years later.

I'd done the Scottish Cup semi-final between Hearts and Aberdeen in April 1996 and they'd won 2–1. After the match I shook his hand, congratulated him, and wished him well for the final, just as I would have done for any manager, but he told me that had stuck with him, and he gained more respect for me as a result.

It didn't stop him giving me pelters on occasion though, and one day when Hearts were at Motherwell and I was fourth official, I decided to take pre-emptive action. I spoke to the kit-man at Fir Park and got some cotton wool from him, rolled it out into two extended cigar-shapes and stuck them in my ears. I picked up the numbers board and the bag of balls, and made my way along the tunnel to the dugout. Jefferies saw me, and instantly knew what message I was sending him. He wasn't happy!

At least I got through to Jim though; that wasn't the case with every manager I dealt with. There were some guys who clearly held a grudge from a decision I'd made years previously, and weren't ever going to let it go. They had formed an impression from one game or one incident – sometimes you weren't even aware of what it was – and they were never going to alter their perception of you. There were managers I dealt with for five, ten years and they carried that sense of injustice with them the whole time.

TERRY BUTCHER (ex-Inverness Caledonian Thistle manager)
We were playing Dundee at Dens Park and I was getting a bit agitated as I felt every decision was going against us and we just couldn't get back into the game. Something else happened out there and I snapped, my frustration got the better of me, and I lashed out with my left arm against the side of the dugout. Unfortunately I crashed it right through the Perspex and left a

gaping hole, which wasn't great for the subs as the wind came whistling through and it got pretty chilly. The compliance officer at the time, Vincent Lunny, issued a complaint against me, but I told them I'd just leaned against the side and it had shattered, and given that there were no witnesses, they had no option but to drop the case. Only now can the truth be revealed!

ALEX SMITH (ex-Stirling Albion manager)

My big thing with any of my teams has always been balance. I drum it into all my players. If we're on the attack, we need to defend properly, we need balance at the back, we need cover, there always has to be the right balance. Balance, balance, balance.

We were up against St Johnstone one day, at their old ground, Muirton Park, and we're 1–0 up shortly before half-time. I'm in the stand, front row of the directors' box, and we get a corner which wee Matt McPhee whips in. Their goalie grabs the ball, throws it out and they're straight up the pitch with their left-back and I see we've got no cover there. He plays in the cross and they score at the back post. I'm straight down the wee turret staircase into the dugout and I'm raging, I'm screaming at my staff, "Every fucking week I go on about balance. Every week! Where was the balance there?"

The half-time whistle has gone and I realise the players are already making their way up the tunnel, but I'm desperate to get to the dressing room first, I want to be in there before them, so I climb out of the dugout again and I'm shoving my way down the tunnel, I'm pushing players aside, hauling them out of my way, because I'm so angry and I want to be waiting for them when they get there. So I get to the corridor and I know the first door is the St Johnstone dressing room, the second is a wee office, so I storm past them and I thump my shoulder against the next door and shove my way in, and I disappeared.

I fell down a set of stairs and landed on the floor of the boiler room. It wasn't cemented, it was just dirt, and I've got on one of those Columbo-style raincoats and a red shirt and tie, and I'm absolutely filthy. I'm lying there stunned, I've hurt my shoulder, and I look up to see eleven faces peering down at me with huge grins on them. So I scream, "What do you think you're looking at? Get into that fucking dressing room!" I pull myself to my feet, and I'm retying my tie and trying to dust myself down, and I hear this voice from the corner, "Aye son, I think you're in the wrang room." It's the old groundsman sitting having his cup of tea, and I'm not in the best of moods. "What the fuck has it got to do with you? Mind your own business!" The old boy takes a sip of his tea, then replies, "Aye, okay son, but don't worry, I see folk doing that all the time."

I get myself tidied up the best I can, and I'm telling myself I have to be composed, I need to go in and control this dressing room, and I walk in and big Andy Graham the goalie is sitting with a towel over his head, he's killing himself laughing and is trying to hide it, but I see his shoulders heaving up and down.

"You lot," I shout. "Every fucking week, every single week, every bloody week in my team-talks what do I talk about? What's the most important thing? Retaining your fucking balance!" Of course I've just fallen down a flight of stairs, so the place erupted, and despite myself, I started laughing too. We laughed for that whole half-time, I never said a word in terms of tactics or the plan for the second half, and they went out and they were brilliant, Robert Duffin was magnificent, and we won 3–1. It was the best team-talk I ever gave!

PETER HOUSTON (Falkirk manager)
We played Hibs at Easter Road, a 3–3 draw, and Alex Smith, who's our technical director, was watching the game from the stand, so that he could get an overview and pass on any comments. He's on our list of permitted personnel in the technical area, so he could come down to offer advice, but he had just had a pacemaker fitted, and I told him beforehand not to go getting

too excited. We've gone 1–0 down, but we get an equaliser back and we're well on top. We score a second, or at least we think we do, but the flag goes up and it's disallowed for offside. Alex is incensed and he comes running all the way down the stairs in that huge stand, and makes his way along to the end of the tunnel. It so happened for this game there wasn't a fourth official appointed, but Alex didn't know that, and when he sees a track-suited figure standing by the dugout, he makes a beeline for him, taps him on the shoulder, and gives it to him with both barrels: "Why are you calling off that goal? That should have stood, there was nothing wrong with it. It's a fucking disgrace!" He's going absolutely crazy. It so happened the guy he had collared was John Doolan, the Hibs coach, but he'd not been at the club long and Alex didn't recognise him.

John was half turned away, still trying to watch the game, so Alex couldn't see the club badge or his initials. He asks, "What are you speaking about? You can't talk to me like that!" And Alex's shouting at him, "I'll talk to you any way I want, you get talking to the ref on the headset, tell him he's got that wrong!"

John's looking utterly confused and then Smithy suddenly realises his mistake, and he's apologising profusely and trying to calm down, and then he about-turns and marches back off up to his seat in the stand. We went in for a cup of tea after the game, and it was so funny, Alex saying how sorry he was and the rest of us killing ourselves laughing.

JIMMY NICHOLL (ex-Raith Rovers manager)

There was a spell when I was player-manager, and I enjoyed that as it meant you could influence things out on the park, check first-hand on players who had picked up injuries, and just generally keep the side organised and focused. It meant that my assistant, Martin Harvey, was in charge of the dugout, and that was fine because he was a good football man, and we could always shout across to each other if either of us wanted to change things.

There was one game against Meadowbank Thistle at Stark's Park, we were well in command and 1–0 up at half-time, and without telling the players, I said to Martin that if we got it to 3–0 he was to substitute me off. Jock McStay got our second early in the second half, and soon afterwards we won a corner. I moved into position about twenty-five yards out, and when a Meadowbank defender cleared the ball it fell perfectly for me. I caught it as sweet as you like, a half-volley with my left foot, and it flew straight into the top corner. Their keeper never stood a chance. The rest of the boys went crazy, partly because I'd actually connected with my left, and Gordon Dalziel and Ally Graham were jumping about celebrating, they were going mental, they couldn't believe it. I just waved my hand at them and said, "Ach, this game's too easy for me. I'll just leave you to get on with it, finish it off yourselves." I walked straight off the park and took my place in the dugout, and of course Martin already had the sub, Ian MacLeod, standing by and ready to go on. The players are now giving me dog's abuse, calling me a big-head, and I just stood there and smiled back at them.

SCOTT BOOTH (ex-Aberdeen)

As a player, the last thing you want to hear shouted from the dugout is, "You've got two minutes!" Willie Miller used those words to me plenty times when he was Aberdeen manager, and so did Jocky Scott. Jocky was a brilliant coach, was great with the young lads, but could be fearsome, and if you messed up during a game, you knew he'd be right in your face afterwards, spitting and breathing all over you as he vented his anger. In a way I suppose it was quite motivational, you'd do everything you could to try to avoid that, and the 'two minute' call from the dugout was, I guess, designed to have a similar effect. Once you got it, you certainly ran about like crazy trying to make something happen to change the manager's mind, but it never really worked with me. In fact, I found it had the opposite effect that

I'd start worrying about taking a bad touch the next time the ball came to me, and I don't ever remember earning a reprieve after the warning had been delivered from the technical area.

BARRY WILSON (ex-Elgin City manager)

Early in the 2014–15 season we were drawn to play Rothes away in the North of Scotland Cup. Now they're one of the weakest sides in the Highland League, but my boys were determined to take the game seriously, so I selected a full-strength line-up and told them we should use the game to score a few goals, and to get the confidence up. That's just how it panned out, and we were cruising, eventually winning the tie 8–1.

Midway through the second half one of their players took down one of mine in the centre circle, and the ball shot across towards my dugout. As it rolled over the line, I controlled it, flicked it up, and volleyed it back on to the pitch for the free kick to be taken, but it flew across, smashed the referee on the back of the head, and pole-axed him. He did a complete face-plant, it knocked him clean out. I turned to look at the linesman and he was just raising his flag, and I said, "Come on, I was a good player, but I'm not that good!" I could have stood there all day and never repeated that level of accuracy! The ref eventually picked himself up, dusted himself down, and started looking around to try to find out what on earth had happened. I raised my hand to apologise and thankfully he took it in good spirit.

STUART McCALL (ex-Motherwell manager)

Towards the end of the 2010–11 season we were at Tynecastle and Hearts were giving us a real doing. They scored again early in the second half to make it 3–0 and their assistant manager, Billy Brown – who's not the quietest in the dugout – was bouncing across the front of our technical area, looking up into the stand, clenching his fists and pumping the air in celebration. As is normally the case, I was oblivious to it all as I was trying to sort out our players, but my staff noticed it, and they weren't at all happy with him. John Sutton got one back for us, and within a few minutes Tom Hateley had made it 3–2, and Kenny Black (assistant manager) and the others are making sure Billy knows we're right back in the game.

With just a couple of minutes left, Gavin Gunning sent in a cross and Sutton headed the ball into the net for the equaliser. They're now pushing to try to win it all over again and as we're defending, one of the lads boots a clearance high into the main stand. A Hearts fan quickly throws the ball back and Billy is moving over to try to get it, but it loops down towards our dugout and Kenny heads it back, further up into the stand again. It was an amazing header, more powerful than most guys could volley, and Billy went crazy. Afterwards he asked Kenny why he'd done it and Kenny replied, "We'd been 3–0 down, we'd got it back to 3–3, and there was one minute left. What did you expect me to do? You'd been dancing in our fucking dugout!" Even Billy had to laugh at that.

BILLY BROWN (ex-Kilmarnock assistant manager)
We were playing against Martin O'Neill's Celtic in December 2002 at Rugby Park. Andy McLaren had scored for us, but they had equalised in the second half, and they were laying siege to our goal. We're defending in depth, hacking the ball clear, because a draw against that team is a great result for us. The game's moving into stoppage time and Jim Jefferies and I are right on the touchline, we're shouting and screaming, we're going nuts, and eventually the ref Willie Young has had enough. When the ball goes out of play he strolls across and says, "There are two men inside this stadium who are acting like two little boys. If you don't sit down and behave yourselves we'll be playing all fucking night. I mean it." We sat down and shut up.

JIM JEFFERIES (ex-Dunfermline manager)
I had various run-ins with referees down the years and some handled the situations better than others, recognising that the

dugout is something of a powder keg, and showing an understanding that emotions can boil over at any time. Willie Young was the best. He'd come across and have a few words, use his sense of humour to calm things down, and that made such a difference. I respected him and could have a laugh, while appreciating that he was in charge. I'd say to him, "Willie you were consistent today, you were rubbish for both teams." And he'd accept that, but you wouldn't get away with that with some of the younger guys, the ones who it seemed were out to make a name for themselves.

We had a Scottish Cup tie down at Stranraer and we were coasting it, 2–0 up with ten minutes left. Willie Gibson played in a cross for them, but he mishit it, and it flew over the head of our keeper Ryan Scully and into the net. So, it's 2–1, and suddenly we're under pressure. The referee, Des Roache, adds on six minutes of stoppage-time, and we're deep into it when they get a corner. We've got everyone back in the box defending apart from Faissal El Bakhtaoui, and I'm desperate to get his attention, to tell him to be ready to get the ball if we clear it, to hold on to it, to run the clock down. I'm shouting at him, and without realising it I've stepped two yards on to the pitch which, to be fair, isn't that difficult down there as it's such a tight stadium. I'm not swearing, I'm not abusing anyone, I'm just trying to attract my player's attention, but the linesman calls over the ref and he sends me to the stand. No discussion, doesn't ask what I was doing, he just sends me packing. As I take my seat, they equalise, and as fate would have it they go on and win the replay at East End Park. The authorities decided not to take any action against me, they showed some understanding, which the referee hadn't.

There was a similar incident up at Elgin the previous year in the Cup, again with a young ref, Barry Cook. It was a filthy day, pouring with rain, slippery underfoot and the wind was howling across the pitch. The referee wasn't having a good game – in fact Ross Jack, the Elgin manager, had just said that to me when he booked our midfielder Josh Falkingham for diving on the half-way line. I marched out of the dugout to the edge of the pitch – which must be a good thirty yards away – and I'm screaming across that Josh had simply lost his footing and that I'd never seen anyone dive there before, if players do dive it's normally in or around the penalty box. The ref came across and said, "Any more of that and I'll send you to the stand." He walked away a few paces, stopped and turned, then added, "In fact, just go there now." I couldn't believe it. Of course we contested it, and when I was up in front of the disciplinary panel I related the full story, and the case was dismissed. Both of those could have been avoided had the officials just shown a bit of common sense, a bit of understanding of the game and what happens in the technical area.

ALLAN PRESTON (ex-Livingston assistant manager)
We were up against Vaduz in the UEFA Cup in 2002 and had drawn the first leg 1–1 in Liechtenstein, Rubio scoring the goal. The home leg was tight, very nervy, and still 0–0 deep into stoppage time when they score. They're celebrating, going daft, and then we all realise the referee has actually blown the final whistle before the ball has crossed the line, he's disallowed the goal, and the 0–0 means we're through on the away goals rule. So now it's us leaping up and down in our technical area, and their coaching staff and subs going mental. Suddenly there's a set-to, and it spills up the tunnel with everyone throwing punches and fighting. It's just beginning to calm down when from the back we hear Jim Leishman shout, "Yis are oot . . . O-O-T . . . oot!" and it all kicks off again. That one took some time to settle down!

BILLY DODDS (ex-Scotland)
It was the second leg of the Euro 2000 play-off against England. We've lost the home game 2–0 at Hampden, and now we're 1–0 up at the old Wembley and pressing for an equaliser. It was the

biggest match I'd ever been involved in, the pressure was incredible and had we done it, it would have been the most amazing turnaround of all time. For some reason wee 'Broony' (Craig Brown, the Scotland manager) shouts at me from the dugout and I run over. He passes on some tactical information and I give him the thumbs up and go, "No bother." I'm running back across the pitch, and I don't know why, but I look back over my shoulder towards him. Now remember, this was a critical stage of the game, and I'm trying to concentrate fully on it, but I find myself watching him retreating to his seat. Unfortunately, he's forgotten it's a tip-up seat, and the next thing I see is Craig flat on his back, his arms and legs flapping in the air as if he was doing that Dead Fly dance; he was like an upturned turtle, and he couldn't get himself back up again. I'm in the middle of this huge match and I'm chuckling away to myself, not quite able to believe what I've just seen. Of course, we go out 2–1 on aggregate, and well after the game once the dust had settled, I got speaking to the guys who'd been on the bench. They said it was so funny, and they were all trying to stifle laughs, but then they heard Craig's voice piping up, "It's no bloody funny!" and that was it, they just lost it completely.

MARK McGHEE (ex-Aberdeen manager)

There was one match at Pittodrie where we felt all the decisions were going against us, and Scott Leitch (the Dons assistant manager) and I were getting more and more enraged, shouting and jumping up and down, going apoplectic at the fourth official. It's probably best that I don't identify the officials as they're both still involved in the Scottish game, but eventually your man between the dugouts can take it no longer and he calls across the referee, who approaches the halfway line, speaks to his colleague and then makes his way down towards our dugout and gestures the two of us forward. We're assuming we're going to be in a bit of bother, which would probably have been deserved given the tirade we'd been delivering, but when we're face-to-face, the ref leans in and says, "Can you tell me where I can get a good curry in Aberdeen?" Trying desperately to keep a straight face and make it look as if I've just been chastised, I reply, "No, but I'll find out for you." He then turns away and gets on with the game. It was a great piece of psychology, it defused the situation entirely and let the fourth official think some form of justice had been handed out, and Leitch and I behaved ourselves for the rest of the afternoon.

ALLAN PRESTON (ex-Dundee United)

Jim McLean was really superstitious, and if the team was leading at half-time he would insist all the substitutes sat in exactly the same seats after the break. He'd be checking just before and he had a great visual memory, so if anyone took the wrong seat he'd go crazy. I've seen games raging on and him ignoring what's happening on the pitch as he was so busy rearranging the subs into the correct order. He'd give you such a bollocking – and trust me, that's the last thing you wanted from wee Jim.

DAVE BOWMAN (ex-Dundee United)

Having spent twelve years at Tannadice, with a fair chunk of it under Jim McLean, there were quite a few interesting experiences as you might imagine. What a character he was; an absolute genius when it came to football and tactics, but it would be fair to say that man-management wasn't perhaps his strong point. He did at least treat everyone the same, he had no favourites.

In my first match for the club he had been berating David Narey from the dugout throughout the ninety minutes, and back in the dressing room he let rip: "Narey, that's the last game you'll ever fucking play for this club!" Now, Davie was a club legend, and I was absolutely stunned, but he just shrugged it off. Of course a week later he was first name on the team-sheet.

I remember Jim screaming across from the dugout to Mixu

Paatelainen one time, "Paatelainen, you're only getting a game because you've got a long throw!" That didn't do much for Mixu's self-confidence I can tell you.

I pretty quickly got used to Jim's antics, both in the technical area and the dressing room. There was one half-time where in a furious outburst he kicked out at a plastic washing basket and his foot went right through it. He was hobbling around screaming at us all, dragging this basket at the end of his leg, and the fitness coach Stuart Hogg was down on his hands and knees trying to wrestle it free. You can't laugh of course, you have to sit there with a straight face and just take the blast. The fans inside Tannadice that day must have wondered what on earth was going on when they saw eleven players head out for the second half all killing themselves laughing and barely able to run in a straight line.

The dugout was not the place to be when Wee Jim was on the warpath, in fact you weren't even safe out on the park, but my former team-mate, the late Ian Redford, came up with a great plan. Ian was deaf in one ear, but he would never admit to Jim which one it was, so when the manager was screaming at him Ian would just ignore him, and when he was picked up on it later he'd just say, "Sorry boss, that's my deaf ear, I couldn't hear you." Jim eventually sent him to the doctor to try to find out for sure which one it was, but he could never remember and Ian just kept on blanking him throughout his United career.

Jim had lots of confrontations over the years, and you were aware of them on occasion as you glanced across to the dugout. I used to love when we were playing against Alex MacDonald's Airdrie or Hearts, because Alex really used gamesmanship and tried to wind him up. Every time Wee Jim went to the edge of the technical area to pass on instructions, Alex or his coach John Binnie would be straight out there screaming total and utter nonsense. They weren't saying anything to their players, just drowning out Jim so we couldn't hear what he was saying, and it used to drive him nuts.

He picked up a few suspensions along the way, and it was a bit of a relief at times knowing he was up in the stand. He would use a walkie-talkie to keep in touch with the dugout, to make calls and changes, and I remember one game at Tynecastle where it didn't quite go to plan. I became aware of the coaches looking up into the main stand trying to communicate by hand signals with the boss, and him doing likewise and looking more and more angry. I found out later that the radio frequency he was tuned into was the same as a local taxi firm, and every time he tried to talk he was getting taxi drivers replying and asking for their next pick-up!

We eventually got a sports psychologist in to assess everyone's mindset for games, and of course Wee Jim was the common denominator. It was agreed he would leave us alone after matches, that there would be a cooling-down period during which he wouldn't come into the dressing room. The first game it was nice and calm afterwards, and we stripped off and went into the showers. Next thing, Wee Jim bursts in, he strips off, and he's straight in giving us absolute pelters in the showers. As far as he was concerned, he'd stuck to the agreement because we weren't actually in the dressing room.

Now that I'm involved in coaching I think back to Jim and how he behaved in the dugout, and I did learn an awful lot from studying him. Many good points, but quite a few I've steered clear of; it's fair to say I'm much calmer in the technical area than he ever was.

DEREK McINNES (ex-Rangers)

I remember one game at East End Park where I was on the bench and Brian Laudrup was having a brilliant match, he was skinning their full-back Eddie Cunnington time after time. He was right on the touchline in front of us, dummied him, feinted, and cut inside and Eddie's gone flying off the pitch and landed on the track again. Bert Paton (Dunfermline manager) came running out of his dugout, bent over his player and shouted, "Fuck sake Eddie, do you not watch *Scotsport*? He does that all the time!" We all just burst out laughing.

JIMMY CALDERWOOD (ex-Aberdeen manager)

Some clubs like to make it as difficult for you as they can – that's all part of the game – but no one did it quite like Hearts under Jim Jefferies. Even before the game they'd have the heating turned up in the dressing room, it would be like a sauna in there, and they'd always say they'd get it seen to, but they never did.

And then once the match started, the moaning began. It was constant, every decision was challenged, everyone was under fire. If it wasn't big Jim, it would be wee Billy (Brown) or John McGlynn. Peter Houston was the only normal one down in the dugout, you could at least have a bit of banter with him, but the others? Oh man! Don't get me wrong, away from the game they were great, wonderful people, but in the technical area during the ninety minutes? A complete nightmare.

Some of their players were just as bad, Steven Pressley chief among them. I remember one game in which we were convinced he'd dived late on to earn a penalty which won them the game and our striker, Noel Whelan, was all for laying him out up the tunnel afterwards. That was one occasion when I might not have stepped in to stop my player getting into bother. There are always people within the game who you get on better with than others, and it's fair to say that Steven and I never really hit it off.

A few years later when I was in charge of Kilmarnock and he was Falkirk manager the two of us played each other on the final day of the season. We needed a draw to stay up, they needed to win. It finished 0–0 and they went down, but that was a really tense afternoon and he was constantly stepping into our technical area and it was pissing me off. I try not to get too involved, so I set Jimmy Nicholl and Sandy Clark on him and he soon got the message!

ALLAN PRESTON (ex-Livingston manager)

I was standing right at the edge of the area one afternoon and the referee, Willie Young, gave a decision against us which I disagreed with. I went nuts, and started shouting and swearing at him. Now Willie was one of the best, not the most mobile, but a great ref, and he saunters over to me until he's face to face with me, our noses almost touching. He asked, "Do you kiss your wife with that mouth?" I'm thirty-four, a young inexperienced manager, and I'm not sure how to react, so I just say yes and he replies, "Well, that can't be very nice for her, can it?" He pulls a Werther's Original out of his pocket, hands it to me, and says, "Stick that in your mouth and shut the fuck up." Then he ambled off leaving me somewhat bemused. It was so clever, a brilliant way to handle the situation, and he defused it immediately.

JOHN McMASTER (ex-Morton coach)

Benny Rooney was the manager at Morton and his assistant was Mick Jackson, the game's not going well, and they're discussing what to do. Big Andy Ritchie's a Morton legend, but he was having a shocker that day and they decide to take him off. He's wearing the number nine shirt, so the board gets held up with the nine on it. Now the dugouts are right below the directors' box and suddenly there's this very polite, softly spoken voice which can be heard asking, "Is that board not upside down, surely you mean to take off the number six?" It's Douglas Rae, who later became the Chairman, and Benny hears this, and of course the rest of the fans are going nuts and screaming and shouting at the manager because he's hauling off their hero. Rooney's doing what he thinks is right to try to get back into the game, he's getting pelters from the supporters and the last thing he needs is a director having his say, so he loses it, turns to the stand and shouts, "Sit on your fucking arse you, and shut the fuck up!" I think Mr Rae got the message!

DEREK McINNES (ex-Morton)

John McMaster always had this thing about one of our players, Michael Deeney, he thought he was soft, and he would refuse to let the physio on to treat him when he'd gone down injured. He'd be shouting at Michael to get up, to get on with the game. One afternoon he'd taken a sore one, and he was lying there in apparent agony. The game's raging on and the physio John Tierney is waiting for it to stop so he can get called on by the referee. McMaster's shouting across for Michael to get up, he's holding on to Tierney telling him he's not to go on, and he's screaming, "You're at it! Get up! Get back on your feet!" Eventually, after a long delay, John breaks free and runs across to have a look at Michael. Turns out he'd broken his ankle! McMaster wasn't bothered, he just said, "Aye, well that's what happens to the boy who cries wolf!"

The manager there, Allan McGraw, was also great fun in the dugout and some of the things he shouted had us in stitches, but he could also get really angry and lose it. We were down at Annan one time, a pre-season tournament, and he got mad at our defender, John Boag. 'Boagy' thought he could play a bit, like Beckenbauer at the back, but he got caught on the ball and Allan let him have it from the sideline. This carried on when we got back into the dressing room and the gaffer's calling him for everything, telling him he's not as good as he thinks he is. As you know, Allan uses walking sticks because of the injuries he suffered as a player and he's standing there letting 'Boagy' have it with both barrels, but as he's in mid-rant, his knee locked and he fell sideways into the hamper where all the towels and dirty strips were. It was one of those big, deep wooden ones, and he falls in slow motion, and as he topples right into it, the lid slams shut and all you can see are his feet and the ends of his walking sticks. Allan's son, Mark, was one of the players at that time and he ran over to help his Dad while the rest of us are helpless, we're pissing ourselves laughing. Mark eventually got him out,

John McMaster went across and straightened his knee for him, and they helped him back up on to his feet, and the funniest thing was he never stopped ranting at 'Boagy' the whole time.

DEREK FERGUSON (ex-Rangers)

I loved playing under Graeme Souness at Ibrox – I was still quite a young player and I learned an awful lot from him – but he could be really tough, really demanding. Generally I'd be out there in the middle of the park, and you'd think I'd have been well away from the manager, and could blank him, but he'd get so excited in the dugout at times that I could hear him clearly, even inside a packed and noisy stadium. His big thing was that you had to play the ball after one or two touches, and if I held on to it any longer he'd be absolutely raging, he'd be turning to Walter Smith (assistant manager) and he'd be shouting at him. I'd be trying to go on a wee run, looking to do something a bit different, and I'd hear him counting my touches, screaming at me, "Five, six, seven . . .!" and he'd be going mental. He'd ask me beforehand to target the key opposition player, their playmaker, and to get to him, but that was never my game. Graeme could do it, boy could he do it, he was a real animal at times, but I never could, it wasn't my way. Funny thing was, when I was a substitute or had been taken off, and I was sitting in the dugout watching him, he'd be taking loads of touches, doing a bit of showboating, strolling around in that style of his. I wasn't allowed to do it, but he was, because he was the gaffer, he was Graeme Souness, he could do what he liked.

WILLIE MILLER (ex-Aberdeen captain)

One day at Pittodrie, I think it was against Hibs, I went in for a challenge and the other player's studs caught my shorts and ripped the crotch clean away. I'm now marshaling my defence wearing what looks like a wee red mini skirt, so I called for a new pair of shorts, and when I get the signal I run over to get changed. Conscious that the fans inside the stadium don't need to see what lurks below, I get into the dugout to slip on the new pair, forgetting that the game was going to be on the telly that night and that the cameras on the other side of the pitch have a clear view of everything that happens in there, so the nation was treated to the sight of the Miller backside that Saturday night. At least I had my jockstrap on.

ALEX TOTTEN (ex-St Johnstone manager)

A game against Rangers at McDiarmid Park became quite infamous and it left me with a criminal record. There was a back-story; our centre-half John Inglis had been sent off at Ibrox in a previous match for elbowing Mark Hateley, and this particular afternoon, in October 1991, Ally McCoist caught one of my players with a similar challenge, but of course didn't get red-carded. I exploded. I'm shouting at McCoist, I'm shouting across to Walter Smith – a good friend – in the other dugout, and it accelerated quickly. I'm bawling that he just buys the league with all the money he spends on players, he's bawling back that we'll never win the league with the rubbish team we've got. This is all just before half-time, and of course it continues on the way up the tunnel. There's a bit of barging, a bit of pushing and shoving, but that was the extent of it.

Unfortunately, the match commander had witnessed it and seemed to want to make a name for himself. Next thing I've got a policeman in front of me saying that he has to take my name and details, and that he's been told to charge me. All 'Watty' and I want to do is get to our players, but we're ordered from the stadium, told we've got to leave. One of the club directors, Davie Sidey, took us up to his house and we sat up there having a cup of tea and watching the Dunhill Cup golf on the television. Walter turned to me at one point and said, "Ethel's going to kill me." To which I replied, "I'm not sure my wife Jessie will be too happy either!" About 6pm we thought it would be safe to head back down, but when we got back to McDiarmid there were reporters and photographers everywhere and we had to run the gauntlet. It was the following May before the two of us appeared at Perth Sheriff Court. I got fined £250 for breach of the peace, while the case against Walter was found not proven. He had Donald Findlay representing him; maybe that helped!

BILLY BROWN (ex-Bradford City assistant manager)
I've been involved in so many incidents, in the dugout and the dressing room, and I do regret them. I'm not proud, I'm ashamed of having done what I've done on occasion. There was one day at Bradford I completely lost it with our striker Ashley Ward. I've grabbed him, I'm screaming in his face, I'm making all sorts of threats and warnings. It was only when I was driving home after the match, and had calmed down, that I thought 'he would have fucking killed me.' That just shows what this game does to you.

CHAPTER FIVE

CHICK YOUNG

For most of the time since its inception, the dugout, or technical area, has been sacrosanct. It has been the sole domain of managers, coaches and players, either those waiting for the call to arms, or those substituted because of injury, poor form, or for tactical reasons.

At most grounds these areas are separated either by the tunnel which leads inside the stadium, or by a demarcation zone of sorts. In recent times that divide has been the home of the fourth official, assorted club employees, perhaps a floor manager (for televised games, the man or woman who gives the referee the go-ahead to kick-off) and the pitchside reporter.

The latter has become a key component of all live broadcasts over the past couple of decades, the eyes and ears for supporters watching on or listening in to commentary of matches. They will foster relationships with managers and players, do the interviews both pre- and post-match, glean any information they can from the fourth official or anyone else nearby, and generally keep a lookout for anything that occurs in either dugout which they can share with the nation.

They are witness to some dramatic occurrences, may on occasion find themselves embroiled in the action as the tensions overspill, and must keep their wits about them at all times.

84

They must possess the ability to think on their feet, and to assess immediately what might be unfolding before their very eyes.

One of the foremost of these reporters is the experienced, legendary and at times infamous Chick Young, who has been wielding his roving microphone and prowling in and around the dugout areas ever since the position was first created.

It is a role he is well suited to, and one he still gets a thrill from carrying out after all these years. It is also one which has left him with an array of stories and experiences that he would not otherwise have encountered.

'It's a really privileged position to be in, in fact I find it quite embarrassing at times when managers turn to me to ask what's happening in another game, or about a decision a referee has just given; it's almost as if you're their first port of call, and I'll often consciously turn and look in the opposite direction if I sense I'm about to be canvassed for my opinion.

'People wouldn't believe some of the conversations that go on in and around the dugout, and quite often things are not what they might seem.

'I was doing an Aberdeen v Celtic game at Pittodrie for the TV one day and beforehand the two managers, Steve Paterson and Martin O'Neill, myself and the referee Mike McCurry were having a blether up the tunnel, and I mentioned to Mike that I didn't want any stoppage time at the end of the game because I needed to get back down the road quickly as I was away in the morning for a week-long golfing holiday with the boys in the Canary Islands. There was a bit of a laugh about that, then we all headed out and I took my place between the dugouts in a little alcove, which was perfect for allowing me to see and hear what was going on.

'So the game gets underway and it's fiercely competitive, the players are kicking lumps out of each other, and Martin O'Neill's out going nuts as is the Aberdeen assistant manager Duncan

Shearer, while Stevie's in his usual position relaxed in his seat, so laid-back he's nearly horizontal. I then hear a voice going, "Chick, Chick . . ." and I assume it's the director trying to contact me so I press the headphone against my ear, but I can't hear anything, and then I feel a tug on my sleeve and I turn round and it's 'Pele' (Paterson's nickname) who's trying to attract my attention. I slip the headphones off and lean towards him, still keeping an eye on the action, and he says, "Is it Las Americas you're going to?" I'm a bit taken aback, and ask him to repeat himself, which he does, and when I say yes it is he asks, "Which hotel are you in?" Now there's all sorts going on out on the park, but Stevie seems quite oblivious, and when I tell him the name of the hotel he says, "Oh yeah, I know it. See if you go out the front of the hotel and go right then right again . . ." and as he's telling me this he's pointing and gesturing the directions, ". . . there's a brilliant wee boozer down there."

'To my absolute horror I hear the commentator Rob Maclean saying, "Well I see our man Chick down in the Aberdeen dugout having a word with the Dons manager, let's find out what tactical changes he's planning . . ." So I have to quickly break off from my chat with 'Pele' and completely off the top of my head tell the nation that he's calling for the right-back to push up a bit further and close down the Celtic winger. It was an utterly surreal moment.

'I've been down pitchside on so many memorable and dramatic occasions over the years. One of the most special was when Scotland beat France in the Parc des Princes in September 2007 with that brilliant James McFadden goal. There was just over an hour gone when Faddy scored and once the celebrations had died down a bit on the Scotland bench, I remember Alex McLeish turning to me, grinning, and with that dry humour of his, saying, "That must be time up, eh?"

'A couple of years earlier I was in Slovenia, and we beat them 3–0 to finish off our qualifying campaign. It had been some game and the goals, scored by Fletcher, McFadden and then Paul Hartley got better each time. Walter Smith was the manager, and after the third he was leaning nonchalantly against the dugout and he turned to me and said, "So, what does the trackside reporter think of this performance then?"

'That was a lovely moment, and I do consider myself fortunate to have enjoyed so many of them down the years.

'Sometimes you do find yourself right in the thick of the action. When George Burley was Scotland manager he had Tommy McLean as part of his backroom team. We were in Macedonia, George in the dugout and Tommy up in the stand getting an overview of the play, and the plan was for him to nip down and tell the manager what he had noticed and to make suggestions. Unfortunately, the stewards didn't fancy that, and wouldn't let him down, so I had to go to the fence, Tommy would tell me the information and I then had to sidle along to the dugout and pass it on to George, and that went on all game long. Not that it made much of a difference, as we lost 1–0. It wasn't my fault though!

'I had a classic with wee Berti (Vogts) too, just before half-time in one game when it looked as if we had scored, but the referee ruled the ball hadn't crossed the line and waved play on. The manager turned to me and shouted, "Chick, Chick, was it a goal?" Now he assumed I had a monitor down by the dugout and had seen a replay, which in actual fact I didn't that day, but I got caught up in the moment and I've got my arms outstretched as I reply, "Wee man, it was this far over the line." He goes absolutely bonkers and as soon as the whistle goes he's down the tunnel after the referee calling him for everything, and got sent to the stand for the second half. I did feel guilty about that one, and apologised afterwards, but that's what Scotland games do to me – I just get swept away in the passion of it all.

'You have to try to avoid that in club football of course, but there are times when the drama is almost too much to cope with. I always remember May 2003 when Celtic and Rangers were neck and neck going into the final afternoon. Celtic were down at Kilmarnock and Rangers were playing Dunfermline at Ibrox, and I was in behind the home dugout. Inevitably some of the coaching staff were looking round to me to check on events at Rugby Park, although they had a pretty good idea by the reaction of the fans around the stadium. At one point there was a roar went up and everyone turned and mouthed through the Perspex to ask what had happened. Up until then it had been easy enough, I'd just been putting up my fingers to signify 1–0 Celtic, 2–0 Celtic . . . but on this occasion it was a missed penalty, Alan Thompson had skied one over the bar. Now, I tried mouthing those words, but they weren't getting it. Have you ever tried coming up with a hand signal to denote a missed penalty? I'm drawing a set of goalposts, I'm raising one hand into the air trying to portray the ball flying over them. Eventually they gave up and just turned their attention back to the pitch. Rangers won 6–1 to clinch the championship by a single goal and afterwards I've left the dugout area and I'm out on the pitch doing the interviews for telly, and the Rangers boss, Alex McLeish, says, "This is really heavy, you couldn't hold it for me for a minute, could you?" Of course, I go yes no bother and reach out for it before reality hits home, and I stop myself just in time. "Aye right!" I say, and he just winks and smiles and heads off on the lap of honour. Can you imagine, with the reputation I've been given over the years, me standing in the Ibrox centre circle holding the league championship trophy festooned in red, white and blue ribbons. That would have been good, eh?

'There was another Helicopter Sunday two years later and this time I was at Fir Park with Celtic, and I got a unique close-up insight into the pressures of the day and the effect it had on Martin O'Neill. Celtic had been leading from early on, and that would have been enough to clinch the title. The longer it stayed 1–0, the more it was getting to him and I stood right beside the dugout watching him prowling around his technical area, kicking

88

every ball, contesting every decision, and then, just as the game was entering its closing stages, Motherwell go and score twice to hand the championship to Rangers and I watched him crumble both physically and emotionally. I actually felt sorry for him that day, getting a sense of what that incredible turnaround did to him. It was really painful to watch, to see the crushing impact it had on the man.

'You do have to be careful mind you, and hide any emotions you might be feeling, but you can still get caught out even in the most innocent of circumstances. I was the trackside reporter at the 6–2 Old Firm game at Celtic Park, and after doing the pre-match interviews took what was my regular position back then, directly behind the home dugout. Celtic ran riot that day, and after one of the goals the camera panned to the celebrations of Martin O'Neill and his staff. Now, I happened to be wearing a camel coat that afternoon and stuck out like a sore thumb among all the green and white, and as the image flashed up on the screen I happened to be looking downwards to check the replay on the monitor, that's what I was actually doing, but to the watching nation it looked as if my head was bowed in disappointment at another Celtic goal. That one ran and ran . . .

'Most of the time it's pretty run-of-the-mill stuff of course, you're watching out for substitutions, for any little flare-ups, but they're generally few and far between. Some managers are pretty laid-back, Stuart McCall for instance would often just lean against the dugout and have a chat, while others have the blinkers on for ninety minutes and wouldn't recognise you even if they were looking straight at you.

'You have to remember that it's a relatively new phenomenon, the pitchside or technical area reporter, and clubs and officials did take a bit of persuading before the role became the accepted norm. I had a problem with the referees for a while who didn't like that I generally had a monitor down beside me and was privy to replays of controversial moments, which meant managers would either turn to me or leave their dugout to have a look for themselves. I know that got discussed at various referee association meetings as they feared they were being undermined by it. And of course the clubs themselves were cautious because they felt having a reporter down there might open up managers or players to further scrutiny. In some cases they were right of course. I remember the Barcelona game at Celtic Park when there was the half-time bust-up. I was standing just by the edge of the dugout and could see it all kicking off up the tunnel. Naturally I reported that to the nation, suggesting that Rab Douglas might not be making an appearance in the second half, and he was indeed sent off along with Thiago Motta. I was only able to witness and report on that because of the license I had to roam the technical areas.

'All in all, it's been great fun doing that these past few decades and I've had some fantastic moments, encountered some remarkable characters, and seen some of the mildest-mannered men on this planet turn into raving monsters for ninety minutes at a time. That's what being in that little marked-off area can do to you – it really can't be good for their health!'

CHAPTER SIX

TALES FROM THE DUGOUT 3

BILLY STARK (ex-Morton manager)

I've always been pretty calm and relaxed in the dugout, but I'm aware that there's this perception from some fans and parts of the media that, as a manager, unless you're jumping up and down like an idiot, you've no passion, you don't care. I've always felt that's a bit ridiculous, that a manager's body language is deemed so important. For me, if you're doing that, you're getting caught up with the opposition, you're not really doing your job, you're losing focus on the game.

Alex Ferguson spent most of his time just sitting in the dugout; it didn't do him any harm, did it? I'm not saying I never lost it, we all have our threshold, but it generally took something extreme at a high-pressure moment for me to snap. One such time came against our local rivals, St Mirren, and it involved their manager, Tom Hendrie. They scored, and he came running across our technical area celebrating. When you try to analyse it later, make excuses, you realise that he maybe just got caught up in the excitement, but it was unacceptable, you don't do that to the opposition. Whether it was premeditated or just spur of the moment, I don't know, but I wasn't happy with him that day, and I certainly told him so. That did get a bit heated.

TERRY BUTCHER (ex-Inverness Caledonian Thistle manager)
We were winning one afternoon, but the game was moving into its closing stages, and I felt I had to make a change to try to bolster things in the middle of the park. I had a conversation with Maurice Malpas (assistant manager) and was swithering over whether to take off Nick Ross or Aaron Doran. We weighed things up, I had another think, and then decided Doran would be the player to go, so I told Maurice and he passed it on to Steve Marsella (coach/scout) who always got the board ready for substitutions. A couple of minutes later I was sitting in the dugout and I'm scouring the park looking for Nick, but I can't see him anywhere, so I turn round and there he is, sat right beside me. I did a double take, and asked, "What are you doing here?" to which he replied, "You've just taken me off." I was a bit taken aback, "No I haven't!" and he just shrugged his shoulders. I shouted across to Maurice and he blamed Steve; Steve was blaming Maurice, and I'm going nuts thinking it might cost us the game. Luckily for them it didn't, and we saw the win out.

SCOTT BOOTH (ex-Aberdeen)
I always remember the first time I stepped on to the Pittodrie pitch and the thrill that gave me. I was still at school, it was towards the end of the season, and there must have been a few injuries and players promoted to the first team, because I got a call on the Friday asking me to join the reserve squad. I was among the substitutes and sat on the bench until the second half, when I got the nod to get ready. I'd been used to playing in public parks, at Harlaw, at Banks o' Dee, and now I was entering the big time, at least that's how it felt.

I remember it was a beautiful sunny afternoon, I remember bursting with pride as I stepped from the dugout on to the pitch, but the rest is a blur. I can't recall who we were playing, I can't remember any details about the match, but one thing that has always stuck with me is seeing the camber on the pitch. It may look flat from the stands, but when you're down there you can see the rise from the touchline to the centre spot, and as I ran on it felt as if I was climbing a mountain!

My senior team debut was also as a substitute, and I remember that better. I'd been sitting on the bench desperate to get the call, and when it came I was determined to get out there and make an impact. Not long after coming on, I cut in from the left and crossed to the near post where Charlie Nicholas headed in his last ever goal for the club. That was such a thrill, and the following week Alex Smith and Jocky Scott put out a young team at Celtic Park – it was the last league game of the season, ahead of the Scottish Cup Final against them – I got my first start, and we came from behind against all the odds to win 3–1. What a start that was to my professional career.

DEREK McINNES (ex-Rangers)

I was among the substitutes quite often at Ibrox, and while that was frustrating, one of the biggest disappointments of my career was the day I didn't even make the bench. It was the nine-in-a-row season and I'd played in every round of the League Cup, I'd scored in the semi-final against Dunfermline, and I played in the games during the build-up to the cup final against Hearts at Parkhead. It was the days of three substitutes, one was always a goalie, so there were two places up for grabs in the dugout and to be honest I never, ever saw it coming. I remember chatting with Charlie Miller before the team was announced and he'd worked out that either himself, Craig Moore or I would miss out, and he suggested we split the two bonuses between the three of us. I never took the bet because it never crossed my mind it would be me. It ended up the two of them started and I never even got stripped, never got near the dugout. Walter Smith had the sub goalie, Theo Snelders, on the bench, he had a striker, Peter van Vossen, and from nowhere, because he had been out injured for a few weeks, came David Robertson.

The gaffer hadn't spoken to me beforehand and I was flabbergasted, I had all the family there of course, because I thought it was going to be my big day. The boys won 4–3 against Hearts, but I didn't want to be involved in any of the celebrations. We went back to Ibrox afterwards and I didn't look at the manager, couldn't speak to him, and then on the Monday I went in to see him. I remember saying to him that I needed an explanation, that while I knew he'd won the cup, I believed that every part of his decision was wrong, that I'd played in every other round, scored goals, that I felt I deserved to have been out there. His response was that Davie had earned his loyalty over a few years and that he thought it important he was involved, that I would have the chance to earn his loyalty in the future, and that on another day it might be me getting the nod over someone else because of that. He then said I'd get the win bonus anyway, and he reached into his drawer and handed me my winner's medal.

I still didn't like it, didn't agree with it, but at least I then had an explanation, and while it was so hard to take at the time, it is something I've used since becoming a manager. My rule is that I will always speak to a player if I'm changing a winning team, if I'm leaving him out. What I won't do is get bogged down speaking to players if we haven't won the week before; I tell them my door's always open afterwards, they can come and see me then, but I won't discuss it in advance.

CALLUM DAVIDSON (St Johnstone assistant manager)

My first game as assistant was in Norway, the Europa League qualifier against Rosenborg. We won 1–0 out there and knocked them out on aggregate, which was an amazing result, but I was new to the job then and didn't fully appreciate just what it entailed. We'd scored early, but they're piling on the pressure, and they force a corner. Tommy (Wright, the manager) turns to me in the dugout and asks, "Who's supposed to be picking up the big number twenty-four?" I tell him I don't know, and he looks at me in disbelief. "You've got the set-pieces list," he says, and I say, "No I don't." "Well you fucking well should have!" he shouts back. I had no idea that was my responsibility, I thought all I had to do was offer a bit of advice and congratulate the boys afterwards, so we had to send the kit-man Tommy Campbell back to the dressing room to get the sheet. I've made sure I have it every match from then on.

WILLIE YOUNG (ex-referee)

I was in charge of a game Aberdeen won 3–2 against Celtic in August 1998. It was some match, one in which I got a lot of head-lines for awarding Celtic three penalties. All the awards were justified, but Craig Burley and Simon Donnelly both missed theirs before Henrik Larsson finally scored late on. They then laid siege on the Aberdeen goal looking for an equaliser and at one point Burley ran past me and shouted, "Any chance of another pen Willie?" I gave him a look and said, "I'd need to take it for you to make it worthwhile."

As you might imagine, the home fans were getting nervous and baying for the final whistle. Hugh Dallas was fourth official – this was back before we were all rigged-up with our communications kits – and he stepped to the edge of the technical area to check how much stoppage time I wanted added on. I signalled five minutes, and he screamed back, "You're joking!" I knew it was the right amount, couldn't understand what his problem was, but the moment he lifted the board with the number five on it, I realised. The supporters in the main stand behind the dugout went mental, they were calling him for everything, baying for blood and going ballistic at Hugh. He had a go at me in the dressing room after, pointing out that the fans had blamed him for the added time and that he'd had to take all the flak, but I just shrugged it off saying that I'd been right, and he just had to accept that.

A couple of months later we were on international duty, a Euro

2000 qualifier between Turkey and Germany, but this time he was ref and I was fourth official. The Turkish fans can be pretty fanatical to say the least, but they were in a good mood when Hakan Sukur put them 1–0 up with about twenty minutes left. Their collective frame of mind changed somewhat when Hugh sent off one of their players soon after, and the Germans were all over them, desperate to get back on level terms. I ventured to the edge of the pitch to check on the stoppage time and saw Hugh smile, then gesture with five fingers. I turned to the assistant, John McElhinney, to check that I'd read him correctly, and John nodded. Now, there was no way there should have been five minutes added on, maybe three at the very most, but I lifted up the board and there was instant uproar. No sooner had the fans behind me seen that glowing number five than I had to hold the board flat above my head like a shield, as cigarette lighters, bottles and flares rained down on me while I ran back to the relative safety of the dugouts. Thankfully, the Turks saw the game out, and when I went across to Hugh after the players had left the pitch, he just grinned and said, "That'll teach you for Aberdeen."

PAT BONNER (ex-Reading assistant manager)

I went to Reading with the late Tommy Burns and after a few weeks he decided the best way for him to see the game and study the players was for him to watch it from the stand, and for me to be in charge of the dugout. I'd be down there, he'd be sat up above, and the idea was we would communicate by walkie-talkie. Now, we'd never used such a system before, and to be honest it wasn't very successful. I never really got the hang of it and Tommy was one for doing a lot of talking and not much listening, and in any case most of the time I couldn't make out what he was saying. I'd have to come out of the dugout and turn to the stand with my hands spread out, mouthing, "What do you want?" We tried a series of hand signals, we even tried shouting back and fore to each other, which was hardly ideal given that the opposition bench could hear everything we were saying. We were getting bemused looks from everyone else in the stand as they watched us try to communicate with each other and eventually he lost patience and decided he'd be better off watching from the dugout after all. That was quite a relief!

STUART McCALL (ex-Rangers manager)

We were due to play Livingston at their place so I'd gone along to see them the game before against Falkirk, and I became very aware of the home supporters giving Peter Houston (Falkirk manager) a lot of stick throughout. There was one voice in particular which could be heard booming out, constantly having a go at Peter, trying to wind him up. A week later, I'm down in that dugout and the guy is there, just a few rows back, bellowing at me all the way through, calling me all sorts. It was an important game for both of us, as we were chasing a play-off and they were fighting to avoid relegation, and it was a tight first half. Right after the break, they score to go 1–0 up and as the celebrations begin to die down, there's my friend giving it plenty: "Ha-ha McCall, your team's rubbish! You don't know what you're doing! You're getting sacked in the morning! McCall, your bubble's burst noooooooowww . . . oh-nooooooo . . .!" And the reason he trailed off was that while he was in full flow, Marius Zaliukas headed in an immediate equaliser for us. I just turned round and gave him a wee smirk, and to be fair to the rest of the Livingston fans, they all had a good laugh about it.

TOMMY WRIGHT (St Johnstone manager)

I tend to try to remain as calm as I can in the dugout. It's not always possible, and there are inevitably moments when you lose your cool, but I learned from one crazy afternoon when I was Ballymena United manager* that you have to be very careful

---

* The incident Tommy refers to is detailed in Chapter Two

how you behave and conscious of how your actions can impact on the players and fans. You constantly hear all sorts of abuse coming from the crowd at away games, but you just have to bite your lip. If you respond in any way you can be guaranteed the fan you've spoken to will be calling for the stewards or police. You should be able to have a wee bit of banter, that's part of the game, but it's just not worth it as even a funny remark can be misinterpreted, or they can claim you've put a swear word in there.

We played Hamilton in January 2015 and James McFadden had been getting all sorts of stick from the travelling fans. When he got sent off in the second half, it got even worse, and as he made his way off the pitch and past the dugout, he gestured to them, a 'get it right up you' salute with his arm. Now, he shouldn't have done it, but that day I could understand why he snapped.

On the whole I've had no real bother with opposing managers, but I have had the occasional incident with the fourth official. That's a really hard job, it can't be easy trying to control the madness that can break out in the technical areas, and I do have sympathy for them, but there are times when they don't help themselves.

We were at Tynecastle, first game of the season, and eventually lost 4–3 to Hearts in a match in which we'd been behind for most of the time, but had fought back to level at 3–3 only for them to quickly snatch their winner. As we were chasing the game, they were constantly wasting time, letting the ball run away at free kicks or throw-ins, delaying the restart, all the usual tactics, and I was getting more and more frustrated. I called over to the fourth official, George Salmond, to make sure enough time would be added on at the end, and he said, "Don't worry, Steven (referee Steven McLean) will look after you." When the board went up, it said three minutes and I was furious. I went back to George and he apologised, and as I turned away again, I threw my hands up in the air in frustration. He shouted me back over and said that while he was happy to talk to me, I shouldn't gesture at him in any way. I suppose he's always trying to please the observer in the stand, and could get marked down under those circumstances, but there really was nothing much to it, no great confrontation, just a natural response at the end of what had been a high-pressure and dramatic game.

IAN MAXWELL (ex-St Johnstone)

Our manager, John Connolly, could be a bit forgetful, for instance he would regularly try to put on a fourth substitute only to be told he'd already used up his allocation. I was on the bench one Saturday afternoon, and we were struggling. We were losing the match and we needed something special to turn things round. The previous week we'd been behind down at Palmerston against Queen of the South and he'd put on Martyn Fotheringham who almost immediately pinged a twenty-five-yarder into the top corner to save the game. John suddenly remembers this and he turns to Jim Weir and says, "Right, get Fotheringham on, same as last week." Jim looks round into the dugout, turns back to the manager, and points out that he hasn't included Martyn in the subs that week. "Oh no!" he shouts, "Who the fuck have I got?" Cue meltdown among the rest of us!

JIM DUFFY (ex-Chelsea coach)

It was back around 2000 and I was studying for my UEFA Pro Licence. As part of the qualification you have to do a detailed analysis of a club; you can pick any one, and I chose Atletico Madrid and planned to do a comparison between them and their city rivals Real. Because I was at Chelsea at the time it was easier to make the contacts, and Atletico, who were coached by the future Chelsea boss, Claudio Ranieri, couldn't have been more helpful. I really was given an access-all-areas pass.

They had recently moved to a new training ground on the out-skirts of Madrid and I was there one morning trying to soak up as much as I could. I was watching on, taking copious notes, and filming with a small hand-held video camera. It was excellent. The players were all in little groups, doing different sessions and working with the various coaches, and I was trying to capture as much of it as I could. I was trying to stay out of the way of course, so I was in the technical area at the side of the training pitch, and as another session started up, I swung the camera round to get as much of it as I could. As I did, I smashed my head off the top of the dugout. It wasn't just a scrape, I burst it wide open. The scar was about an inch long and right at the top and in the middle of my head, and being bald, there was nothing to stop the blood. Instantly it was spurting out and running down my forehead and into my eyes and mouth. I must have looked like an extra from a B horror movie, the lunatic Scotsman with the bloodied face!

I reached into my pocket and found a hankie, wiped what I could, and then compressed it on to my head. I'd also taken the precaution of bringing along a baseball cap to protect my skin from the sun, so I then wedged it on top of the hankie and rather sheepishly approached the club doctor. Fortunately he'd spent time in Scotland and spoke perfect English, and he took me to the medical room and patched me up with four butterfly stitches. There was me trying to make an impression at one of Europe's biggest clubs, a team packed with international superstars, and I've made a complete fool of myself. I was due to go out for dinner at a posh, upmarket restaurant that night with their director of football, the legendary Paulo Futre, and some of the rest of the staff, and I knew I couldn't go looking as I was, so I went to a chemist to try to get some skin-coloured antiseptic cream. Try asking for that when neither of you speaks the other's language! Anyway, I got some, blended it in and tried to hide the stitches and the wound as best I could, and thanks to some helpful dimmed lighting in the restaurant, I got away with it. At least I think I did, they never asked about my head, maybe they were just too nice or diplomatic to bring it up. That scar is still there, clearly visible, to this day.

JIM JEFFERIES (ex-Hearts)

When I was a player at Tynecastle, the trainer was the club legend John Cumming, and he was such an inspiration to all of us, a real hard man, a real football man. We all loved him. The dugouts back then were the old style, sunk into the ground so that your eye line was at pitch level, and made of brick and with a solid roof, nothing like the fancy Perspex structures these days. John was unbelievable to sit beside as he played the game from the bench, he just couldn't sit still, he was forever moving about, kicking every imaginary ball. One afternoon I was a sub and sitting alongside him, and there was a cross came in from the wing and Drew Busby leapt to head it. As he did, so did John, and I heard a dull thud. When he sat down again, I dared to look round and saw blood trickling down the side of his head and past his ear. He'd smashed his head against the roof and I suggested he'd better go in to get it stitched, but John saw himself as indestructible, and would have thought it a sign of weakness to leave the game at that point. There was only about ten minutes gone, so for the next thirty-five he sat holding a sponge against his head, occasionally squeezing the blood out of it into his water bucket. He even had to go on to the pitch to treat players a couple of times so he just ran out with the sponge clamped against the wound. He finally got it stitched at half-time.

On another occasion we were playing Motherwell at Fir Park and John was as jumpy as ever on the bench. One of our guys went in for a slide tackle and John copied him. As his leg shot out, he tripped up the Motherwell sub Colin McAdam who was out warming up, and sent him sprawling on the track. John just looked at him and said, "Sorry son," and carried on watching the game. Thankfully big Colin saw the funny side of it!

Ahead of one big match, we'd been training all week with John and the manager, Bobby Seith, and Bobby had been working particularly with the full-back Jim Brown on his overlapping. He wanted Jim to bomb forward, but that we shouldn't give him the ball, 'He's only a decoy' was the message the boss repeated every day. That sentence, 'He's only a decoy' got drummed into us over and over again. He wanted Jim to distract the other team while we opened things up infield. Just before kick-off we were out on the pitch and John calls to us from the dugout. A few of us go across. "Remember, dinna gie Jim the ball, he's only an escort!" shouts John. We had barely stopped laughing in time to start the game.

ALASDAIR ROSS (assistant referee)
The best insult ever directed at me was at Tynecastle. I'd been down by the corner flag and was making my way back up towards halfway. The Hearts fans were less than enamoured by a decision I'd just made and I was running the gauntlet, they were all booing and jeering me. As I stopped just in front of the dugout I very clearly heard one supporter behind it loudly call me 'a fat, gay, lesbian bastard'. It so happens the guy was sitting just along from some guests I'd got tickets for, and one of my friends shouted back, "He'll be really upset at you calling him fat."

NEIL SIMPSON (ex-Aberdeen)
I've discovered over the years that the dividing line between success and failure in this game is such a narrow one, that there are defining moments in every player's career. Mine came right at the start. We were playing Hibs at Pittodrie and I was on the bench, and at half-time Alex Ferguson gave me the nod and told me I'd be going on to replace Andy Watson. As you might imagine I was very excited, bursting with anticipation, determined to go out and make the most of my chance. Within a minute, the ball came to me and I let it run under my foot and out of play, and all

I heard was this explosion from the manager in the dugout. That didn't exactly help my nerves, and the next time I was passed to I also mis-controlled it and I could feel Fergie's eyes boring into me from behind. I was having a nightmare. But shortly before the end I picked up the ball, drifted past a couple of opponents, and fired a long-range left-footed shot into the top corner. That moment gave me all the confidence I needed, convinced me I could make it at the top level, but it might all have been very different.

JIMMY NICHOLL (ex-Cowdenbeath manager)
One of the most remarkable games I've ever been involved in during my career was against Stirling Albion at Forthbank in March 2011. It was also the most unprofessional I've ever been during a football match. As a manager, you have to be thoroughly prepared and totally organised ahead of each game. One key thing is when you're making a substitution; the player going on must be made fully aware of his responsibilities, and that's why you'll always see an assistant manager or coach talking to them, showing them a piece of paper, as they wait for the go-ahead. That's all about ensuring they know where they should be positioned and who they should be marking when defending corners and free kicks. It's a basic point, but it's very important, and every manager will ensure that's done.

We were getting thrashed, 3–0 down with thirteen minutes to go, and I was totally fed up. I turned to my bench, pointed at three of the subs – Scott Linton, Greg Stewart and Marc McKenzie – and I told them they were going on, not to bother warming up, just to get their tracksuits off. My assistant, Colin Cameron, was still playing at the time and he was one of those I took off. He came across shouting at me, couldn't believe he'd been subbed, and I'm telling him he'd had a terrible game, that he deserved it. Meantime, the guys going on are asking who they should be picking up, and I explode, telling them it doesn't matter, they can do what they want, the game's finished. It was complete and utter mayhem in that technical area. Within seconds, Mark Ramsay cracks one in from thirty yards, 3–1. They get a man sent off and concede a penalty, Ramsay scores again, 3–2. With a minute left, Archie Campbell equalises and deep into stoppage time Greg Stewart scores another. It was unbelievable. 3–0 down with thirteen minutes to go, a complete shambles in the dugout, and yet we go on to win 4–3.

We get back to the dressing room and wee 'Mickey' (Cameron) is still arguing about why I took him off, when the chairman, Donald Findlay, breezes in to congratulate us all. The players were bouncing around going, "What about that?" and I had to stop them in their tracks, tell them how unprofessional I'd been, and that I'd learned two things that day. Firstly, never underestimate the importance of the next goal in any match, and secondly, the game is all about the players. I'd got it horribly wrong in how I behaved, and yet somehow we went on and won the match.

It's all about attitude, and I got a further reminder of that when I went to see the Albion manager, Jocky Scott, and his assistant, John Blackley, for a beer afterwards. I went into Jocky's room and he told me that John had been so angry he had gone through all their players, savaged them, then stormed out of the stadium saying he was never coming back again. And he never did.

TERRY BUTCHER (ex-Motherwell manager)
It was a pre-season friendly against Cowdenbeath at Central Park, but it was absolutely freezing, the wind was howling across the park, and we were all huddled-up in the technical area in our big coats. It was unbelievably cold! The dugouts were fixed into the ground at the back, but loose at the front, and all of a sudden I heard a bang, and spun round. The wind had whipped the whole dugout up and flipped it over on to its back, and before anyone could move a muscle, another huge gust from the opposite direction had sent it flying back into its original position. It

had all been so quick, none of us could react, and we were all left looking at each other as if wondering 'did that really happen?' It was like the visor of a crash helmet being flipped back and then forward again. Thankfully no one was hurt, it could have been so dangerous. Because I find it hard to squeeze into some of the smaller dugouts, I often stand up just at the front, and if I had been that day I might have had my head knocked off.

ERIC BLACK (ex-Metz)
When I moved to France from Aberdeen I was determined to immerse myself in the culture and to properly learn the language as quickly as possible. I knew I'd make mistakes, but I decided to go for it as I felt that was the best way to pick things up. We weren't that long over there when we discovered my wife, Nina, was pregnant, and of course I wanted to tell my teammates the good news, so as I had to do at that stage, I thought through what I wanted to say and practised it over and over in my mind. After training one day, we were all assembled in and around the dugout waiting for a team-talk, and I decided to take my chance. Having got the lads' attention, I proclaimed, "Ma femme est enceinte." Or at least I thought I had. They were all smiling and telling me not to worry, that I was in France now, that anything goes, that it was fine, no problems. I was a bit confused until it became clear that because of my terrible accent and pronunciation, they thought I'd said 'ancienne' and not 'enceinte' and that I was telling them my wife was ancient!

STEVE TOSH (ex-Arbroath)
I didn't spend too much time on the bench when I was playing in the lower leagues, but my first ever experience as a professional player was in the dugout, and it's one that's stuck with me to this day. I'd had a few offers from other clubs, but signed for Arbroath, who had Jocky Scott in charge then. It seemed incredible to think he was there; just a few years earlier he'd been at

Aberdeen, had won the cup double, and nearly the league title, and you could see he found being in charge of a part-time club all a bit frustrating.

I remember my first training session. It was at Gayfield, it was pouring with rain and the wind was whipping across the ground as usual. Jocky set up a corner routine and the boys were trying to play the ball into a certain area, but they were slicing it over the bar, kicking it off the park. Eventually, he said, "This is what I'm wanting," wandered over, and clipped a perfect corner to the exact spot he'd highlighted. It must have been difficult for him working with players who weren't up to the standard he'd been used to in full-time football.

Anyway, that first game was at Central Park against Cowdenbeath and I'm one of the subs. I'm just a raw youth, the two other guys were hardened senior pros who had done the rounds, and I'm sitting there too scared to move. I'm thinking I should go for a warm-up, but I don't want to do so before they do, I'm waiting to take their lead. It hadn't been the best of games, it was pretty scrappy, and after about twenty minutes I turned to look at the manager, who was leaning against the side of the dugout. I see him shake his head, and talking to himself, he utters the immortal phrase, "What the fuck are you doing here?" I look back now and it seems funny, but then, all excited about making my debut, it completely deflated me. Into the second half, it's still 0–0, and my big chance comes, and the last words Jocky says before putting me on are, "Go out and enjoy yourself, and change the game for me." I certainly did. Within thirty seconds of me taking to the park, big Mark Yardley scored to make it 1–0 them, the only goal of the game. Jocky quit the job soon after, I think he only had about fourteen games in charge.

STEVEN THOMPSON (St Mirren)
Supporters wouldn't believe how often players forget the most simple and basic items when they're among the substitutes. I've

lost count of the number of times a teammate has pulled off his training top to reveal that he's forgotten to put his shirt on! Shin-guards are the worst though, that's a regular occurrence, and leaves the kit-man or someone else scrambling around trying to find a replacement pair. The sub goalie is usually the man to turn to as he's least likely to need his. It's incredible how often it happens, I mean it's hardly rocket science, there's not that much to remember. What do I need? My kit, my shinnies and my boots; but I've been guilty of it just like everyone else. The other regular one is the manager, coach or player banging his head on the dugout, either in celebration or anger. It happened more with the old fashioned dugouts, and if it was the gaffer and he's really whacked himself, it took a lot of self-restraint to stop from bursting out laughing.

I've worked with a lot of managers, and there were some you might have got off with that, but Tommy McLean certainly wasn't one of them. Of all my bosses, he was definitely the most ani-mated in the dugout and lost the plot so many times. There were games where you couldn't concentrate on the play as you were so wrapped up listening to Tommy's constant ranting. One thing that is always guaranteed to raise a laugh in the dugout is when the manager and his assistant go into full *Chewing the Fat* mode. The boss runs out and starts shouting and gesturing, and his number two follows him and starts shouting the same things and making the same moves. I know Phil Neal got some stick for that after the TV documentary showing him in the dugout with Graham Taylor when he was England boss, but I can assure you he's not the only one who's done it. And Taylor's not the only manager who screams from the edge of the technical area and gets ignored by his players. That's happened with me many times; if you know all your gaffer wants to do is give you a rollicking, to slag you off, you're not going to spend much time trying to listen, are you? You just blank him, cup your hand to your ear and pretend you can't hear him over the noise of the crowd!

SCOTT BOOTH (ex-FC Twente)

John van't Schip was brought in as coach and he and I never got along, he wasn't my cup of tea at all. He had something of a playboy reputation, Marco van Basten was his best pal and I remember him bringing Marco into the stadium one day and it was as if he was showing off. I always felt he saw the Twente job as something of a stepping stone, that he wasn't there to try to improve us as players, to pass on his undoubted experience and help us, it was all about him. I played regularly throughout much of my four years there, but not during his time in charge; that was a period when I had to get used to sitting on the bench. I was there one night for a KNVB Cup tie at the Amsterdam Arena, which is a stunning ground, and I wasn't in the best of moods because once again I'd been named among the substitutes. We were playing the Ajax second team, Jong Ajax, which plays down the divisions, and they were giving us a humping. That team was full of seventeen and eighteen year-olds and they destroyed us, can't remember the score, but they beat us very easily and knocked us out of the Cup.

I'm sitting there watching on, I'm pissed off because it's becoming clear I'm not getting a game, and I'm bored. It wasn't the right attitude for a professional, but everything had got to me, and to be honest, I was sulking. They've got these big Perspex dugouts at the stadium, I'm sitting in the corner, and I decide to make myself comfortable, so I gather together some bibs and those big warm coats, and I make a kind of cushion for myself. I didn't lie down or anything, I just leaned a bit to the side with my hand by my head and got comfy, and stayed like that until the end of the match. I never thought anything of it until the next morning when I picked up the papers and the headline news is that I'd fallen asleep in the dugout during the game! There were pictures of me looking relaxed, but certainly not sleeping, however it grew arms and legs, it made the news across Europe from what I gather – 'substitute falls asleep during match' – and was picked up by the Scottish media too. It got completely out of hand, it was crazy. I even had the assistant manager come up to me and ask if I'd been sleeping, he took me aside and quizzed me about it, and I had to remind him that I'd been sitting right next to him and pointed out that he might have noticed had I been grabbing forty winks! I know how stories can grow arms and legs in the game, but that one was just ludicrous.

JIMMY CALDERWOOD (ex-Dunfermline manager)

We were playing Celtic in a Scottish Cup tie at East End Park, and as I always like to do, I was wandering around the pitch before the end of the warm-up having chats with the individual players. I began walking across to our midfielder Ian Ferguson – who we had of course signed from Rangers – and before I get to within fifteen yards of him, he's raising his fingers and shouting loud enough for the away fans to hear, "What's that gaffer? Nine in a row!" and he's dancing around in front of them. The Celtic fans were baying for blood, so I just shook my head and walked across to the safety of the dugout.

The game itself was a cracker, it finished 2–2, Larsson scored twice for them and Barry Nicholson equalised for us in the last minute, but Fergie was living on the edge throughout, and in fact the referee, Willie Young, probably should have sent him off. There was one particular flashpoint in the middle of the park and it was all kicking off. I'm at the edge of my technical area, shouting across and trying to calm things down, but Fergie's having none of it, he's going ballistic. All of a sudden I hear him screaming at Willie, "You're supposed to be one of us!" Thankfully it was Willie in charge, one of the experienced guys, and he sorted it all out. If it had been one of the younger refs it would have been a straight red, and the situation would have got even worse.

I always liked Willie, and others like Bobby Orr and Hugh Dallas. They used humour and banter out on the pitch, or down in the dugouts when they were fourth official, and you could talk to them. I know they've got a difficult job, and I know us managers make it more difficult at times, but they handled things really well, knew how to defuse situations, and there was definitely a mutual respect that grew between us. We understood the pressures of each other's jobs.

John Rowbotham was another, he was brilliant, and while I had a few run-ins with Kenny Clark, he was also very good. I met him at a function recently and he was digging me up about something I'd done years ago. I couldn't even remember it, but it had obviously stuck with him, and we had a good chat. He told me he loved refereeing my teams because of the way they played the game; I told him I hated it when he was in charge! We had a laugh about that, but I'm not sure you'd be able to do that with some of today's officials; it's a different world.

BILLY STARK (ex-Queen's Park manager)

We were playing Cowdenbeath at Central Park – which is some place – and Mixu Paatelainen was in charge of them at the time. I got on well with Mixu, I'd taken him to St Johnstone, made him my assistant and got him into the coaching, so what happened really surprised me. They absolutely humped us, it was 6–0, and near the end of the game the ball came off the park and ran towards him as he stood near the dugout. He went as if to knock it back to one of my players, but then took a step and let it run between his legs and away down to the side of the track. It might seem like a minor thing, but it's disrespectful, especially when you're winning a game as easily as he was. I spoke to him afterwards and he held his hands up, apologised, but it just shows what can happen down there, even in a situation in which his team was in total control and there was a friend in the other technical area. You just get caught up in the moment.

One thing I would say about the dugout is the difference between being an assistant and a manager down there. When you're the number two you think it's just going to be a wee step up to being the boss, but you honestly haven't got a clue. The difference is like a million miles to being the one standing there with all the responsibility on your shoulders.

DAVID VAN ZANTEN (ex-St Mirren)
I was among the substitutes for a game at Firhill against Partick Thistle and they were awarded a corner early in the second half. We're leading 1–0 at the time and they push most of their big guys up hoping to get an equaliser. Our boss, Danny Lennon, is straight out of the dugout, and he's screaming, "Who's picking up Balotelli? Who's marking Balotelli? Someone get on Balotelli!" Of course he means Conrad Balatoni, but has got the names mixed up, and we're creasing ourselves at the thought of Mario Balotelli playing for Partick Thistle. Danny glances round and as we all try to cover up that we're laughing at him, someone points out that Balatoni hasn't even gone up for the corner, he's standing on the halfway line. That was it, we were gone, and there are howls of laughter from the dugout as the boys clear the danger out on the pitch. Danny's standing there absolutely bemused; he had no idea what he'd said and why we were cracking up.

DEREK McINNES (ex-Bristol City manager)
We had a game coming up against Crawley, so Tony (Docherty) and I had gone to watch them against Oxford. It was when Steve Evans was in charge, and we found ourselves unable to concentrate on the match, we became obsessed with what was happening in the dugout. He was so confrontational, he'd wound the opposition manager up so much that he'd got the other guy sent off, players were being sent off, and it was all as a result of how he was behaving in the technical area, the indiscipline all stemmed from him and what he got up to down there. He caused Oxford to completely lose their composure.

So before our game with them, we made a big play about it, we said their players would try to wind our guys up, they'd stand over the ball, they'd kick it away, they'd feign injury. I said that Evans would be arguing throughout, he'd be wanting to fight, he wanted to make it that type of game, but my guys weren't to respond to that, weren't to react, we were better than that.

Within five minutes I've lost it, he's like a red rag to a bull. He's been contesting every decision, he's been trying to shout louder than me, and he got right in my face, he's got me hook, line and sinker. I'm at the edge of my dugout, I'm calling him for everything, and he's standing there laughing. He knows he's done me, I've fallen into his trap. We had a drink and a laugh about it after, but at that point in the match I'd completely lost it. He's a one-off, not everyone could pull it off, but that's how he works and it's certainly been effective for him.

BARRY WILSON (ex-Elgin City assistant manager)

It had been a really stormy game down at Stranraer, March 2011, and we were 2–0 up. Our boss, Ross Jack, and the Stranraer manager, Keith Knox, had been nipping away at each other all the way through, winding each other up. Every time they played the ball through, Ross would shout, "Ah, the long ball again!" and it was in danger of all kicking off. The dugouts there are right on the touchline, it's all very tight, and there's always the potential for a bust-up. We play a through pass down the wing and Craig Gunn's after it, and he gets taken down by the linesman! It was crazy, never seen that before, but the linesman was about two feet on to the pitch, he got caught out by our quick break, and he's brought our player down as he was setting off towards their goal.

As you might imagine, all hell broke loose! I'm normally pretty placid down there, but I lost it, and I'm on the pitch pointing to where the incident took place, and shouting my mouth off. The referee comes across and shouts to me, "How dare you enter the field of play!" And he sends me to the stand. I just step in behind the dugout, but he's not happy with that, and eventually the police come and escort me up into the main stand. I think I got the equivalent of three sendings-off for that!

Meantime, Ross and Keith are at each other again, and before I know it Ross is up sitting beside me – he's been sent off too – and we've got no one in the dugout to look after the team. They got a goal, and they laid siege after that, both sides had a player sent off, the home fans were going mental, but somehow we held on to win the game 2–1.

SCOTT BOOTH (ex-Borussia Dortmund)

Not long after joining Dortmund I was named in the squad for FIFA's Intercontinental Cup against the Brazilian side, Cruzeiro. I was one of the substitutes and didn't get on, but it was an experience just sitting there on the bench. Throughout the game I was aware of a fancy sports car sitting behind one of the goals, in fact it got hit by the ball a few times, and I kept wondering why it was there. The whole time I'd glance over from the dugout and see it sparkling there in the floodlights. Eventually I got told it was the man of the match prize, put up by the sponsors, Toyota, and whoever won it could decide whether to get it shipped home from Japan or take the cash equivalent, which must have been forty or fifty grand. We won the game 2–0 and Andreas Möller was picked as top player, so I asked him what he'd do. He said, "I don't need another car, I'll take the money." It was mind-blowing, it really was, just a whole different world for me. I'd just left Aberdeen a few months earlier and if you got named man of the match there, you'd be lucky to get a bottle of whisky!

JIM LEIGHTON (ex-Aberdeen goalkeeping coach)

Our management duo of Craig Brown and Archie Knox could be quite an entertainment in the dugout, with Archie in particular likely to go off on one at any moment. We'd been going through a pretty tough time, results hadn't been great, and on this afternoon in particular the team had been struggling. Archie was getting more and more heated-up and eventually he snapped, "That's it, I've had enough. I'm making a sub, I'm making a fucking sub!" He picked who was going on and called over the kit-man, Jim Warrender, who started to get the board ready. Jim asked which number was coming off and Archie replied, "Any fucking one you want! I don't care, it's up to you, just get one of them off!"

PAT BONNER (ex-Republic of Ireland)

It was the qualifying campaign for Euro 96 and we were away to Liechtenstein. I was among the substitutes that night and it was a tiny ground. There were only a few thousand fans there, it just had the one small stand, and there were no proper dugouts as such, so we were all crowded together on a long, uncomfortable wooden bench. It was Jack Charlton's last year in charge and it was a really tight group in which we were battling with Austria and Northern Ireland for the runners-up spot behind Portugal, so although we were up against the minnows of the group, it was a really important match and the pressure was on. We were murdering them, and I mean murdering them. We were all over them, had all the possession and were peppering their goal with shot after shot, but we just couldn't score. Jack was standing at the edge of the dugout and when yet another chance was missed, he turned and let out a roar of frustration before spotting a spare ball sitting in the technical area. He let fly and booted it towards where we were sitting and as we ducked for cover the ball smashed off the edge of the bench and flew back over his head, bounced a couple of times on the pitch, and came to rest in the centre-circle. No one quite knew how to react, but eventually the referee stopped the game, picked it up, and brought it over to our area where Jack had to sheepishly admit what had happened and apologise profusely.

DUNCAN SHEARER (ex-Scotland)

I won seven caps for my country, scored on my debut against Finland, and those are among the most cherished memories I have of my playing career, but there was one of those appearances I could have done without. It was the game after the one in Helsinki and we were in Moscow to play Russia in March 1995. It was the first time I'd ever been there and the trip itself was incredible, there were so many eye-opening moments, a real culture shock I suppose, but it was bitterly cold, absolutely freezing, the whole time we were there.

On the night of the match the temperature had dropped further, it must have been sub-zero, and it was blowing a hoolie. I was one of the substitutes and I went out now and again to do some loosening off, but in the main it was all about huddling in the dugout and trying to stay out of the cold and wind. The boys were doing well, it was 0–0 late on in the game, and I was quite happy to stay on the bench with all my training gear and my big jacket on. I was at one end of the row of seats and the manager, Craig Brown, was at the other and I see him looking along, so I turn away trying not to catch his attention, but I hear the words "Get the big man ready, I'm putting him on." I'm thinking surely not, we're fine, we're drawing away to Russia, a point's a good result, why do you need to put me on? But I get the shout and as I'm burying my head in my hands and going, "Noooo . . .!" the rest of the subs, Brian Martin, Nicky Walker, Stephen Wright and Billy McKinlay are all pissing themselves laughing. Now, I'm as patriotic and proud a Scot as you can get, but there are limits even for a Highlander, and that night in Moscow stretched them. Anyway, I get stripped off and on I go, and I even managed a couple of shots at goal, but it was a nightmare trying to get up to the pace of the game in that cold and even after such a short time out on the pitch, I was delighted to hear that final whistle, couldn't get up the tunnel and back into the dressing room quick enough!

DEREK McINNES (ex-West Bromwich Albion)

Gary Megson was my manager there, he was something of a tempestuous character and lots of people didn't get on with him, but I did, I liked him, and he placed a lot of trust in me. I was his captain, and it's fair to say, probably his favourite, he loved me as a player. We were losing 1–0 at Carrow Road against Norwich City and as I came off the pitch, he called me over to the dugout and said that he was going to go right through me in the dressing room, but that I should ignore everything he said, that none of it was meant. That's just what he did. In front of all my teammates, he slaughtered me, said that Norwich were running the midfield, that I was a disgrace, that I wasn't playing like he needed a captain to play. He tore me to shreds! We were much better second-half, drew 2–2, and he came up to me afterwards and explained that he'd done that to provoke a reaction. The rest of the players knew how he rated me, and if they saw he was prepared to do that to me, he hoped it would push them on because they'd want to avoid it happening to them. I pointed out it had got a bit close to the bone – it did hurt me a bit – but he just laughed it off, reminding me it had all been an act.

He was always looking for something to give him, give us, an edge and he came up with an incredible ploy on the final afternoon of the 2001–02 season. Manchester City had already been promoted and it was in our own hands to join them. We were neck and neck with Wolves and needed to beat Crystal Palace in that last game at The Hawthorns. We're in the dressing room, and as you can imagine it had been a pretty tense week, we're feeling the pressure. Gary took centre-stage: "It's important you do this for the club, it's important for the fans and yourselves, but these are the people it's most important of all for, do it for them." At which point the door was opened and all our wives and children came spilling in, our kids running up to us and cuddling us, and it completely broke the tension. It was a touch of genius. Honestly, we'd have beaten anyone that day!

A few of the Palace lads had been on the wind-up during the week, saying they'd prefer to see Wolves go up rather than us, but that was never going to happen. Megson's last words were, "Leave this room as Championship players, return as Premiership players." We were so fired up. In the tunnel, one of our lads, Darren Moore, went storming up to the front, grabbed the Palace striker Clinton Morrison by the throat and issued dire warnings as to what he was going to do to him during the match. It was completely out of character for Darren, but that was the frame of mind he'd been put in. After watching that unfold, Davie Hopkin (Palace's Scottish midfielder) turned to me, laughed, and said, "You guys look a good bet to win today." We did, 2–0.

ALEX McLEISH (ex-Aberdeen)

Alex Ferguson used to say to us as young players that while growing up we had to 'evolve on the pitch'. He'd tell us there were some things he couldn't teach us, things we had to learn to deal with ourselves while we were out there, but that never stopped him berating us from the touchline! You'd be getting on with your game, concentrating on what you had to do, and you'd hear this roar from the dugout: "Alex!" It was something we discussed as a squad in the dressing room, the fact that he was killing us at times with his constant shouting, so we decided to evolve right enough. He hated it when you didn't acknowledge him, and he'd just keep on going until you did, so we learned that if you just turned and waved towards the dugout, that was him kept happy and he'd go back and sit down again. That's what we did, we hardly ever actually heard what he was trying to say, we just looked over and waved, a kind of 'you're right gaffer, got that' nod, and thankfully he'd leave us alone.

I do remember one game when neither I nor Willie (Miller) were playing and Doug Rougvie was made captain. Big Dougie loved that, he was very proud, and he spent much of the game organising everyone around him. The manager would shout across and Dougie would turn to the boys and say, "I'd better go over and get the instructions to pass on to you." This carried on throughout the match until he got the shout once again and he loped over to the side of the pitch, turning to the boys to make sure they could see what was happening, that he was carrying out his role with great importance and authority. He leant towards the dugout and cupped his hand to his ear waiting, he assumed, for some vital tactical advice to be passed over. All the manager said was, "Rougvie, come aff." The look of astonishment on his face was a picture, he did a double take, and then just stepped over the touchline and took a seat on the bench.

CHAPTER SEVEN

GORDON STRACHAN

There are numerous managers who put on a show when patrolling their technical area, men who offer a form of entertainment quite apart from what is happening out on the field of play.

But few are worth watching more than the Scotland boss Gordon Strachan.

A skilful, confident ball-playing midfielder whose teasing runs tormented defenders across the continent, Gordon avoided physical confrontation as best he could, instead deploying his razor-sharp wit to try to defuse situations on the pitch. That approach has served him well as a manager; he sees humour as a release valve to the pressures of the game, pressures which he says intensify in the dugout.

'You really have to be down there to fully understand what goes on, what it's like to be in that confined space as you try to do your job, to win matches. The fans, the media looking on might think they've got an idea of what it's like, but they don't. Unless you've actually been in that dugout during a high pressure game, you can't begin to imagine how it feels.'

Strachan began his managerial career with Coventry in the mid- to late-1990s while still playing. He had to endure successive relegation battles before finally succumbing to the drop in 2001 and was sacked early the following season. He took over at Southampton soon after, revived their fortunes, and led the club to the FA Cup Final in 2003 before taking a sabbatical to recharge his batteries.

That turned out to have been a good plan, as his next job could hardly have been more intense; for the next four years Gordon was in charge of Celtic, leading the side to three successive SPL titles, League Cup and Scottish Cup triumphs, and back-to-back appearances in the last sixteen of the Champions League.

He had taken Garry Pendrey to Celtic Park as his assistant manager, and retained the services of club legend Tommy Burns, installing him as first team coach in addition to his youth development role. It was a decision which was to prove fruitful in many ways, and provide more than a few laughs in the Celtic dugout. The two men shared a similar sense of humour, and got on well. Gordon has often spoken about the impact of Tommy's death in 2008, and what he contributed to their successful time together. He held Burns in the highest regard, but the coach didn't always get things right.

'We had been deliberating, Garry and I, over a substitution and we finally decide we're putting Shaun Maloney on to replace John Hartson. We've weighed up the options, and we're happy that's the right course of action. So I've asked Tommy to sort it out and he nods. I'm explaining to Shaun what I want, that he's taking over from John, and that I want him to go on and do the job John was doing, he has to play the Hartson role. As this is going on, there's a break in play and Chris Sutton comes across to get a drink of water. I see him there, then I turn to speak to Tommy, and when I hear the referee blowing his whistle I look back at the pitch to check that Shaun is in the right position. What I see is Shaun standing beside John Hartson with his arms outstretched asking what he's supposed to do now. He's quite perplexed given that the man he thought he was replacing was still standing next to him. I do a double take, look back at the bench, and there's Chris Sutton sitting having a drink of juice. "What are you doing there?" I ask him, and he replies, "You've just taken me off." I'm a bit stunned, and say, "No I haven't. I never took you off." This goes back and fore, with him insisting I had just subbed him. I turn to Garry and he just shakes his head, he's having nothing to do with it, so I look along the dugout and Tommy is now hiding behind it, with his hand covering his face. He'd only gone and taken off the wrong player! Shaun's face was a picture, he's completely baffled, and shouts across, "I thought I was being John Hartson!" so I call back, "Could you now be Chris Sutton?"'

Tommy Burns was loved by everyone at Celtic, adored by the fans, and held in high esteem right across the world of football. Strachan says he was an integral part of the management and coaching structure at the club, and was never short of a word or two of advice, particularly in the technical area. But their exchanges were not always what they might have seemed to everyone else watching on.

'Tommy was brilliant. He would regularly come up to me in the dugout and cover his mouth with his hand and whisper in my ear, and people would assume it was all sorts of magical manoeuvres or tactics, but he used to come up and say just the stupidest things, you wouldn't believe some of the things he said. He made such a big thing of it, leaning in all conspiratorial and covering his mouth, that everyone thought it was a really important message he was passing on.

'I remember my first Old Firm game at Ibrox and I was getting dog's abuse. It couldn't have gone any worse, I'd made a bad start as Celtic manager, we'd been knocked out of Europe by Artmedia losing 5–0 over there, we'd drawn 4–4 with Motherwell, it was still early in the season and we were 2–0 down to Rangers with minutes to go. I heard this singing all around the stadium, 'Chesney, Chesney what's the score?' (Strachan was given the nickname by Rangers fans based on a character from the television programme *Coronation Street*) and I'm oblivious to it. I'm thinking what on earth is going on here, and Tam can see I'm confused, so he sidles up to me and whispers, "It's fucking you. You're wee fucking Chesney." He would just pitch his tent up at the other end of the dugout Tam, come across and say something stupid, and then disappear again.'

In season 2007–08 Celtic had made it out of the group stages of the Champions League for the second year in a row. Having lost out to AC Milan in the previous campaign, they now faced the might of Barcelona and twice led the Catalans at Celtic Park, only to lose 3–2 to a Messi- and Henry-inspired comeback by the visitors. The second leg at the Nou Camp would therefore be a daunting experience.

'I did the big speech before the game. We get there, and it was the usual manager's diatribe about keeping it tight, shutting them down, not giving them room to play, hold them out for as long as we could. The longer it goes, if we're still in it with twenty minutes to go we'll panic them – ha, panic them, that'll be right! Anyway, I've done all that, so out we go, down the tunnel, fantastic atmosphere, and we've not touched the ball and they score, the ball's in the back of the net. What a waste of time that was. So, I'm standing there at the edge of the dugout, and I'm feeling completely on my own. He comes creeping up, his usual thing Tam, and I've thought "he's going to help me out here, just reassure me that everything's going to be all right, because he's been here with Celtic before." But no, he comes up, covers his mouth, and whispers, "I've found a trap-door at the back of the dugout. If you want to use it, use it now." He was such a funny guy, just brilliant.'

Earlier in that campaign they had beaten Shakhtar Donetsk in a tough group match at Celtic Park, a game in which Gordon was less than happy with the tactics employed by the Ukrainians.

'They were horrible that night, and after the game the folk watching on telly saw me walking from my dugout and shaking hands with their coach, Mircea Lucescu, and the commentator's giving it, "Look at that, after a game like that the two coaches are warmly shaking hands and congratulating each other on their team's performances." I watched it back later, and I'm thinking, "No, that's not quite what I was saying to him." What I actually said was, "You're the biggest lot of cheaters I've ever seen in my fucking life." He kind of smiled at me, but I think he knew what I was saying all right.'

The following season Strachan's Celtic were taking on another of the game's giants, Manchester United, in a group match at Celtic Park. It was an intense affair, a high-pressure 'Battle of Britain' encounter which had gripped the nation, and once again Tommy served up the dugout humour which had Gordon laughing on the sidelines despite the enormity of the occasion.

'I miss him so much, I really do. We're playing Man United and we had Cillian Sheridan up front, that's how well off we were. They've got Berbatov, Ronaldo, Giggs, Vidic and it's 1–1, it's a magnificent score. It's late on and I'm now putting on a young striker called Ben Hutchinson. We had to take Cillian off, he couldn't run any more, and we're up against it, we can barely get out of our own box. Of course the crowd are roaring us on, "Come on Celtic!" and I'm really not sure how to get through these last ten minutes, what do we do? I asked Garry, and he offered a few suggestions, then I stupidly asked Tam. Now, he's always at the bottom end of the dugout, to my left, so he's come up and I've told him I'm under pressure here, I've no' really got a clue what to do, I'm running out of ideas. So again the hand goes up to the mouth and he leans in, "You think that's bad? It's fucking worse than that," he says. "What do you mean?" He pauses for a moment, looks behind him, back at me, then whispers, "The blind punters over there, even they're giving you stick. They think you're fucking rotten and they can't even see the game." I looked at him, that smiling face, and I said, "Eh? It's 1–1 with just a few minutes to go, and anyway, how do they know what's going on?" But I turned round towards the stand, and right enough there was one guy giving me dog's abuse. I just burst out laughing. Moments like that with Tam were so important in the dugout, they helped you to step away from the madness that's going on around the pitch. I don't think he meant it, it wasn't a deliberate move to ease the pressure; he just thought it was funny at the time. But what it does do is just help to clear the mind, to break that cycle of constantly assessing all the players, trying to work out how to change things, and allows you to take a deep breath and refocus. Honestly, he was brilliant, he was absolutely brilliant.'

Gordon has always tapped into humour as a way of coping with the pressures of top level football, and the dugout has provided many such occasions for him during his time in management. There have also been incidents which have rendered the normally sharp and articulate Strachan almost speechless. One such moment came during a game at Tynecastle where, having complained to the police commander about Hearts fans banging on the roof of his dugout and hurling abuse at him, he was given the advice, "Just you be quiet and watch the game."

Another came in a Scottish Cup tie at St Mirren Park in March 2009. Celtic were involved in a tight head-to-head with rivals Rangers in the race for the SPL title, and had just nudged ahead following a narrow midweek win at Kilmarnock. Prior to that, the side had dropped points in three successive league matches, but had rediscovered their form in a 7–0 thrashing of the Saints seven days earlier at Celtic Park.

Despite that, the manager was feeling under pressure – he would quit the job at the end of that campaign – and he wasn't helped by a bizarre incident that dismal afternoon in Paisley.

'We hadn't been playing well, life wasn't great at the time and we were at St Mirren. There were grey skies, the rain was lashing down and there was no proper roof covering the dugout area. I'm getting soaked, I'm feeling miserable and I'm wondering what on earth I'm doing there. We were 1–0 down (Saints would go on to win the match thanks to a Billy Mehmet penalty) and life doesn't get any worse than this, it just doesn't get any worse than this, I really shouldn't be doing this for a living, I'm useless, we're 1–0 down to this lot. The Celtic fans are singing, "You're getting sacked in the morning!" and the St Mirren fans are laughing at me, they think it's hilarious. I'm thinking of ways to get the game stopped, I'm thinking of faking a heart attack, that might save me, anything just to get out of there.

'I've looked at the dugout and I've thought there's no' much there, it's no' inspiring, can't put anybody on, and just when I think it can't get any worse I see this figure out of the corner of my eye, and he's walking down the tunnel. He's got a St Mirren tie on, and I'm thinking 'where's he off to?', must be going to their dugout to check something. Suddenly he's tapped me on the shoulder, and I've turned round, and I see all the subs looking round from our bench, and we're all wondering what's coming next. And he says, "Gordon, em, just to say, have you got the keys to your dressing room? I want to put the sandwiches out now." I went, "You fucking what? I'm about to get the sack here, it's pissing with rain, it doesn't get any worse than this, and you want to know where the keys to the dressing room are? Do us a favour and fuck off will you?"

'There are two policemen behind us and they can hear everything that's going on, and I turn to them and say, "Get him out of here before I go bonkers will you?" The players on the bench are all now laughing and I'm absolutely raging. I can't believe it. He goes away, but five minutes later he's back and I'm going, "Naaaaw!" The two policemen's eyes are lighting up, they can't believe he's going for it again, and he says, "I'm sorry about that Gordon, but the other week the away manager gave me dog's abuse for not having the sandwiches in after the game. I'm just making sure they're there for you." I couldn't believe it, the game's carrying on, we're losing, I'm under pressure and he's going on about the sandwiches. I asked him, less than politely, to get lost.

'So we get beat 1–0, we're out of the Scottish Cup, it was a horrendous day. I get back to my flat and I'm sitting there thinking this is as bad as it gets. Mark McGhee's just along the road, I know what I'll do, I'll go along and see him and he'll make me feel a bit better. So I'm sitting there with Mark, having a cup of tea, we're chatting away and I start telling him this story, and as I do I can see a kind of smirk coming across that big face of his, and I don't have to finish the tale. I'm about halfway through and I stop and say, "You were the other away manager, weren't you?" And he just smiled and said, "Yup. I was the other manager." That just capped off a perfect day!'

Gordon says he rarely got involved in disputes in the technical area, whether with the opposition, fans or officials, but he did find himself drawn into situations involving his loyal assistant, Garry Pendrey. 'Garry was usually the one who got more excitable than me and I used to try to help him out by calming him down, but somehow I always seemed to bear the brunt of it.'

One such incident occurred in August 2007 during a match against his former team, Aberdeen, at Pittodrie. It would ultimately lead to a two-match touchline ban for the then Celtic boss, but he maintains to this day he was the innocent party.

'It had absolutely nothing to do with me and in fact the steward in question later wrote to me apologising and saying he had got over-involved. Aberdeen did everything they could to make my life a misery at the time, they sent people down to the disciplinary hearing to say I did all sorts to try to make sure I got a suspension, so I was quite annoyed about that. It all kicked off because there were guys in the stand putting their fingers up to Garry going 'one-nothing' when they were in front, so when we came from behind, he turned from the dugout and lifted his fingers to show the score, 'two-one'. Earlier he'd been getting on fine with them, feeding them sweeties, but when he did that someone complained to the steward – who was about thirty yards away – that he'd given them the V-sign. So, he came shooting down and he's pointing at Garry threatening to get him ejected. I got fed up with it, suggested he get back to what he was supposed to be doing and let us get on with the game. He's still nipping away, the fourth official calls over the referee, and I got sent off for that, which wasn't funny, but it was a recurring theme; Garry gets involved, I get punished.'

Strachan can be a stubborn individual, particularly when he knows he's in the right, and one such occasion led to another sending-off when he was in charge of Southampton.

'At the start of the season I'd checked the rules and they'd changed them so that two people could be standing out in the technical area, as long as only one of them was in a forward position. Garry was behind me and I was at the edge of the area, and I hear this fourth official – who I never got on with – telling me to sit down. I reply "No" and he repeats the demand. This went on for a while, 'Sit down . . . No' and eventually I didn't even bother turning round, I just stood there staring forward and going, "No. No. No. No." He calls the ref over and I get sent off. Couldn't believe it! So, I go to the disciplinary hearing and I get off with it, because I was right.

'That was all down to the fourth official being determined to mark me out. Look at the lower divisions in Scotland – they don't have fourth officials for the games there and there's never a problem. Managers there can mumble under their breath, 'He's the worst referee I've ever seen in my life', but if you've got someone standing behind you, monitoring you, he hears that and the ref immediately gets shouted over. Does it really matter to the referee that I've said that? I do think fourth officials are a problem, I don't think they're any use whatsoever down in the dugouts and anyway if something does kick off, there's always a policeman nearby who can step in.'

Some managers have tried to foster relationships with officials, perhaps to buy themselves a little leeway during heated moments in the technical area, but Gordon has never been one to employ that tactic.

'No. Look, you shake hands with them, wish them all the best, but that's as far as it goes. I actually feel sorry for the guys doing the fourth official role, they probably don't want to be down there either, but I guess it's a good living, they're probably better paid than about ninety per cent of Scottish footballers.'

Gordon Strachan was a superb player, winning a catalogue of domestic and European honours, and an undoubtedly successful manager, particularly with Celtic, but he's always been honest enough to admit his failings, and to accept there have been times when he felt he had no answer to the challenges thrown up by the game. One such occasion came against Manchester United at Old Trafford when he was boss of Coventry City.

'You prepare your team before a game, you tell them this is the stage for them, this is where they should be playing, that they can trust their teammates, they're ready for the challenge, blah, blah, blah . . . but as they're going out of the dressing room door you're thinking, "this lot are rubbish, give me my lucky tracksuit." So I've got all my lucky gear on in the dugout, but within no time at all we're 3–0 down and I think I'd better get out to the edge of the technical area and start waving my arms around, do all those signals you see managers doing, look like I know what I'm doing. But it's carnage, absolute pandemonium out there, twenty minutes gone. As I'm standing there, goal four goes in and I can see Mr Ferguson staring across going, "Yeaaahh, I've got you, I'm going to rub your face right in this." So Garry Pendrey comes out and says, "What are you doing?" and I tell him I'm just doing the signals stuff to make it look like I'm in control, basically I want the players to think I'm still with them. As he turns away, I shout to him, "Garry, do us a favour, find out what the record score in the Premier League is, will you?" So he goes away, and of course there you've got to walk up the steps, it's a fair height, it's a fair distance away and I see him returning to the dugout. So I'm still out there feeling like the loneliest man on earth, and I'm still waving my arms and making all these signals and gestures, and for some reason there's a lull inside the stadium, honestly you could hear a pin drop. And all I could hear, in fact everyone could hear, was, "Gaffer! Gaffer!" So I turned round, and Garry yells out, "It's nine! The record's nine!" And I'm going do us a favour, keep it quiet, and all I could see was the Man United dugout looking across and they know exactly what I've been thinking. I'll be honest, I've had better days than that one.'

Strachan smiles ruefully, and then laughs as he recalls another incident on the opening day of the season a few years later.

'I was at Southampton and we were losing to Leicester, so I wasn't in the happiest frame of mind. I had this rule that no-one was allowed a mobile phone in the dugout, so when I hear one ringing I turn angrily to the bench where everyone pleads innocence. I'm issuing threats, I'm saying whoever's done that won't be going on another trip, I'm going to have them. After a while it starts ringing again, and again I turn to glare at the coaches and subs, and it's only at that point I feel the phone vibrating in the inside breast pocket of my jacket. I never did own up to that one.

'I've also done the usual one where you turn to one of the subs and say "go and get yourself warmed up" and you're met with blank stares and confusion, a quizzical look. I'm thinking "why doesn't he want to go on?" and Garry leans in and tells me I've already made the three substitutions. That's happened twice in my career. There was another time at Southampton when I was considering making a change and I look back into the dugout and I see our striker Agustin Delgado sitting there. He was right at the back, he had a hat on, a scarf on, an overcoat and gloves, and he's drinking a cup of tea. It was at QPR, we were playing Fulham there when they were ground-sharing, and we're losing, so I say to Garry, "I wish I'd listed Delgado in the subs today, we could do with putting him on." Garry says, "He is a sub today." So I look back at the player and I say, "Well he's certainly fucking disguising it well, he's never been out for a warm-up, he's drinking tea and he's wearing glasses. How am I meant to know he's a sub?" We actually came back and got a draw that day, our keeper Antti Niemi went up for a late corner and hit the bar, and we equalised from the rebound. So I race out of the dugout on to the pitch celebrating, and when I turn round there's this woman just beside it and she screams over, "Hey Strachan, you little wanker, get off our pitch!" I walk over and say, "For starters, it's no' even your pitch, you're just borrowing it." She went bonkers at me!'

That is by no means the only time Gordon has had a 'discussion' with supporters housed around the technical area, and he admits his patience has been stretched on a number of occasions.

'Some of it is not easy to take. There is a sense of humour there, but what I've found is that it only works one way; the fans think they're being really funny, but when it's the other way about, I'm being "abusive", so you need to watch what you're doing down there.'

As outlined earlier in Chapter One, the former Scotland boss Craig Brown takes a very studied approach to the dugout and has firm guidelines about how players should look and behave there. Strachan has a more relaxed outlook.

'I love Craig, and Andy Roxburgh to death, but I've got a different attitude to them in that respect. I remember being subbed-off against France one night, in fact it was the night Andy came away with the immortal line, 'their centre-forward is just a poor man's Joe Jordan'. It just so happened to be a young Eric Cantona – he did all right, didn't he? Anyway, we got battered three-nothing, I was rotten, I got taken off, I'm sitting there on the bench and it's raining, I'm miserable, I'm thinking it's the end of my Scotland career. We're back in the dressing room after and Andy asks Craig if he's got anything to say. 'Broon' says yes he does, and I'm thinking come on, give me something here, give me some hope, a crumb of comfort, and he went, "I was just speaking to the observer there and he says that's the smartest dugout he's ever seen." I couldn't get close enough to him to get my hands round his throat at that time, but I'm sure my look gave away how I was feeling: "Oh, for fuck sake".

'I remember another time in Romania, we were heading to training and I always liked to have my socks rolled down for that and big Roy (Aitken) liked his pulled up. Andy and Craig insisted that everyone looked the same, so they told us we had to find a compromise before we began. There was a stand-off, but eventually we came downstairs at the correct time, each of us with one sock up and one sock down. "That's typical of you

Strachan!" was all Andy could say. Those two were crackers about the look of the dugout, the appearance . . . Do us a favour! Can you pass a ball? That's what really makes a difference to a team.'

For much of his career Gordon operated on the right touchline and was therefore the first point of contact for the managers and coaches he worked under. There were plenty occasions when the information was useful, important in trying to alter the outcome of a match, but there were others when it bordered on the ridiculous, and caused the winger a real sense of frustration.

'I lost it with Bobby Gould once when he was Coventry manager. He'd been on at me all match and eventually I snapped and gave him dog's abuse. Never a good idea. Even worse was the time at Aberdeen I told Alex Ferguson his tactics were useless. We were in Romania, we'd beaten Arges Pitesti 3–0 in the first leg, but we were 2–0 down in the second and it wasn't even half-time. The manager had decided to play three up-front that day, I'd never played like that in my life before and I was lost, we were all lost, didn't know what to do. He was going ballistic from the bench and I shouted back at him, told him in no uncertain terms it was all his fault. I've never seen a whole dugout react like that. Their faces were frozen in shock and they're all thinking, 'What's he doing? He's just committed suicide!' Archie Knox was just shaking his head, and he's going, "Noooo!" I couldn't concentrate for the next fifteen minutes, knew what was coming, and so I took as long as I could walking slowly into the dressing room to take my bollocking at half-time. That was the game the tea urn got knocked over and tea cups were flying all over the place in there. He really wasn't a happy man that day. Anyway, I went out second-half and I scored a penalty – talk about pressure! – that got us back into it, and we drew 2–2 to go through comfortably in the end.

'I had some scary moments like that, but also a lot of fun,

and quite often those revolved around the assistant managers I played under. Mick Brown was Ron Atkinson's number two at Manchester United, a lovely man, but when you threw pressure on him he got spooked. One afternoon, just before the game started, I ran across to Mick in the dugout and said, "Mick, I can't make it, my ankle's killing me." Now Ron used to sit up in the stand, so it's just Mick down there, and he's getting flustered, he's spluttering and panicking: "What am I going to do?" Then I go, "Nah, it's okay, I'm only kidding, see you later!" and I run back on to the field with him shouting behind me, "You bastard! You Scots bastard!" I ended up scoring that day.

'Mick Hennigan was another, he was Howard Wilkinson's assistant at Leeds, and he was brilliant with me. There was one game when our defence cleared the ball and I see him at the edge of the technical area waving us upfield and shouting, "That way!" Then the other team knocked it forward and he's waving in the opposite direction: "Back lads, back!" Then we counter and he's waving us forward again: "That way now, that way!" So I've had enough of this, and when the ball's over the other side of the pitch, I walk off and up to the dugout, I bend in, and I say, "I've fucking got it Mick. If the ball goes that way, I go that way, and if it goes the other way, I go the other way. Okay?" And as I'm walking off he shouts, "Aye, you're too fucking quick for me Strachs, too clever, but some of these fuckers need help out there!" Mick was good, I loved him, he was so funny. Another one he did, and you see lots of coaches doing it, is that gesture where they move their hands up and down in front of their chests and make exaggerated breathing noises. He's standing at the edge of the dugout doing that one day, and as I pass I call across, "I've got the hang of it Mick. I either breathe, or I die!" He really was some boy, looked like old Steptoe. I had great fun with him.'

As a manager, there was a spell when Gordon would sit in the stand to watch at least part of games and he acknowledges you do get a much better view up there, but he says there are good reasons why bosses need to be down in the dugout most of the time.

'When I went to Celtic for instance, I was getting dog's abuse for the first three weeks, and it looks as if you're hiding when you go up into the stand. I needed to be out there, let the players see I wasn't shying away from anything. I still think it's better to be up there, and that's why I've got Mark (McGhee) there for Scotland matches. The only problem is you're not supposed to be in contact by walkie-talkie or phone during international matches, so any time he sees something, he's got to come running down to the dugout to pass on his thoughts.'

The period Strachan refers to above came right at the start of his period as Celtic manager. It would prove to be a highly successful reign, both domestically and in Europe, but it began in excruciating fashion in Slovakia. His team were taking on the unheralded Artmedia Bratislava in a Champions League qualifier, and by the time the shell-shocked boss walked from his dugout at the end of the ninety minutes, his side had been dismantled by five goals to nil.

'Oh, that's the worst, easily the worst, and touch wood I'll never experience anything like that again. As I've said before, I'll have inscribed on my gravestone, 'At least this is better than Bratislava'. The whole thing was a farce. Bobo Balde missed training because he had a gap in his contract allowing him to talk to other clubs, and being as arrogant as he was, he thought that meant any time and didn't bother turning up. Chris Sutton smashed his cheekbone early on and had to go off, Aiden (McGeady) missed one from under the bar to give us a goal at least. Everything you could possibly think of went wrong that night. I think they had six attempts at goal and scored with five!

'It was a long night in that dugout I'll tell you. It's a testing place the dugout on nights like that because the cameras are on you. I mean honestly, you think 'what am I doing here?' Life was good, I was doing *Match of the Day 2*, I could go and play golf, was having a lovely time – what was I thinking of! Must be mad, must be absolutely bonkers. We're walking out of the dugout afterwards and Garry says to me, "I think we might have to take a few slaps before we get it right." And he wasn't wrong! But he was good Garry, very important at times like that. He would go crazy in the technical area during games, but outwith that he was very level, nothing really affected him, and as a manager you need that kind of backing. That was some night, some experience. But I survived, I survived.'

CHAPTER EIGHT

TALES FROM THE DUGOUT 4

SCOTT BOOTH (ex-Scotland under-15 coach)

There's always that bit of banter down in the dugouts between coaches, and while I try to stay as calm as possible, inevitably there are times when it all kicks off. We were playing Russia in a tournament and I had a disagreement over something pretty minor with their manager, but it escalated, we're giving each other the stare, and we're squaring-up to each other, albeit it at a distance from our own technical areas. I shouted something then dismissed him with a wave, and turned to walk back across to my dugout when a ball came whistling past my ear, must have missed me by a centimeter! Had it connected, it would have floored me. I turn round angrily and he's standing there, hands in pockets, whistling away innocently trying to pretend it was nothing to do with him, while my kids on the bench are trying desperately not to burst out laughing.

There was another game that sticks in my mind, but for entirely different reasons. It was against Portugal and when I took my place in our dugout, I glanced round to their one as you do, to size up the opposition, give him a nod of acknowledgement. What immediately struck me was the guy's massive beer gut. It was incredible! Not just that, he was clearly very proud of it and had on a tight-fitting T-shirt which he'd rolled up to expose this expanse of flesh. Honestly, it was like a huge pregnant belly hanging out over the top of his trousers, and I kept feeling compelled to look round at it. At times it was difficult to focus on the game. He was so animated, jumping around everywhere, and this stomach was wobbling and bouncing as he did. Fair play to him, he was obviously very happy with it, and his boys loved him, they had a great team spirit and genuinely celebrated with him after the game. I've seen and experienced many things in football, but that was a first, and an image, no matter how hard I try, that I fear I will never be able to erase from my memory.

ALLAN PRESTON (ex-Livingston assistant manager)
We were playing Kilmarnock at Almondvale and our Spanish defender Oscar Rubio played a ball up the line and was caught late. To be honest, there wasn't much to it, but him being him, he made the most of it. The Killie assistant Billy Brown was out of the dugout like a shot and he's bawling at Rubio, so I go racing across and within seconds Billy and I are in each other's faces. I love Billy, I've got great respect for him, but it carried on and as we're going up the tunnel at the end we're throwing punches and trying to do each other. Ten minutes later it's calmed down and we're sharing a beer – that just shows how for those ninety minutes, anything goes!

ERIC BLACK (ex-Aberdeen)
Working under Alex Ferguson was quite an experience, especially for a young player like me. You never knew quite what was coming next. I once scored a hat-trick at Celtic Park and got bollocked in the dressing room afterwards! Out on the pitch you were constantly aware of him watching on from the technical area, and if you made a mistake, you daren't look round in the direction of the dugout. Mind you, he wasn't slow in letting you know that you'd angered him; you'd hear that voice bellowing out and you'd be dreading going back inside after the game, or at half-time.

He ruled by fear, no question about it. One example of that came early in my career; I'd had a good start, I'd won a couple of trophies, I was just nineteen and everything looked great. The manager called me over to the dugout one Friday at the end of training and said that I was to get a new contract and that I should go to see him the following Tuesday. I'm immediately shitting myself! I didn't have an agent, so I phoned my Dad, but he was a fitter in the construction industry and hardly experienced in the ways of negotiating football contracts. He simply told me to think it through, be sure about what I wanted, and that he would back me all the way. So, all weekend I'm mulling it over, trying to work out just what to ask for. A car, better bonuses, a signing-on fee? I've got it clear in my mind, I'm ready, or at least I think I am.

On the Tuesday he shouts over, 'See me after training!' and my legs buckle. I get showered and changed and I walk along towards his wee office. I'm gulping for breath, trying to get my mind straight, and I stand outside thinking, 'Car, bonus. Car, bonus.' I knock on the door and there's no answer. I wait a bit, knock again, and I hear, 'Come in.' I open the door and I walk in, and I stand there. He doesn't even lift his head. He's sitting at the desk writing on a bit of paper as I repeat over and over in my mind, 'Car, bonus. Car, bonus.' He gives that wee cough of his and growls, 'Sit down' and I crumble on to the chair. He never even looked up, he never said another word. He simply turned the piece of paper round and slid it across to me. I didn't even look to see what was on it. I just lifted the pen, signed the contract, and said, "Thanks gaffer." I'd signed a four-year deal, no car, no bonus, just a few quid a week more, but I got out of there alive!

STEVE TOSH (ex-St Johnstone)
I've worked with so many different managers over the years, some of which I have more respect for than others. There were

those who were very focused in the dugout with no room for any humour down there, and there were others who played up to their gallery, put on an act for the fans. I didn't like that; it was clearly all very manufactured, and I found it difficult to take those guys seriously.

Throughout my career there have been lots of bizarre and amusing incidents in the technical area, but the one that sticks with me most of all was potentially critical, one that was really scary at the time. We were playing Dundee United at Tannadice and our manager was Paul Sturrock, a United legend who had been one of the stars of that highly successful side under Jim McLean in the late 1970s and 80s. Our midfielder Gary Farquhar had suffered a bad injury early on, I think he'd broken his leg, and after a delay for treatment and to get him off the pitch, we had to make a quick substitution, with Mark Proctor going on. Soon after, Jim Bett scored to put them ahead and it seemed everything was conspiring against us. When you're on the bench and you let in a goal, the natural thing is to look to the manager. In a perverse kind of way, although you're supporting the team, you're hoping there's going to be a benefit for you. You think you should have been playing in the first case and now you're hoping you might get the chance.

Roddy Grant was the other sub, and I clearly remember the pair of us looking along towards the other end of the dugout. Normally Paul would be going crazy after we had conceded a goal, and so would his assistant John Blackley, but there was no reaction this time, and we could see something was going on. Paul then collapsed, he slumped down in the dugout, and the physio ran to him. It was surreal, very frightening, and to be honest the rest of the afternoon was a bit of a blur. I remember them rushing him away down the side of the pitch, and in fact he was put into the ambulance that had come to take Gary Farquhar to hospital, so Gary had to wait for another one to arrive. We got snippets of news throughout that evening and the suggestion was he'd had a heart-attack, but thankfully that wasn't the case, and it was later said he'd got overexcited and had hyperventilated. It wasn't until the Monday morning back at training that we got the full story, and it was such a relief, but that day will live with me forever.

WILLIE YOUNG (ex-referee)

I don't have the best memory in the world, so throughout my career I kept a notebook with details of every match I'd officiated at. I had a look back through it to remind me of a few tales for this book, and it was quite an experience, one that gave me all sorts of flashbacks – some good, some less so. It reminded me that my first major occasion as a fourth official was the 1995 League Cup final between Aberdeen and Dundee – no major incidents that day – and also of the number of Old Firm encounters at which I was stationed down between the dugouts. I was fourth official for at least ten of them, and some were pretty crucial games, but surprisingly there were no serious flashpoints at any of them. I guess the Celtic and Rangers managers over the years realised the potential consequences of any misbehaviour, that they were under the spotlight at those games, and so as far as they could, kept the histrionics to a minimum.

I was reminded of a League Cup tie at Celtic Park where, after a 1–1 draw with Partick Thistle, Celtic eventually won 5–4 in the shoot-out, a scoreline which took eighteen penalties to produce! Neil Lennon took one of the worst spot kicks I've ever seen that night. He stubbed his toe on the pitch as he went to strike the ball and the Thistle keeper actually had to walk forward from his line to pick it up as it bobbled towards him.

One name features large in that notebook, and that is the former Rangers manager, Dick Advocaat. I was fourth official at the 1998 League Cup final between St Johnstone and Rangers – Hugh Dallas was in charge – and at the time the competition was run by the Scottish Football League and teams were listed by numbers one to eleven rather than season-long squad numbers. The SPL sides had the option throughout the competition to use either, and on the day of the final at Celtic Park, Saints went one to eleven and Rangers didn't. I hadn't thought anything of it, and Rangers clearly hadn't noticed, because when St Johnstone were awarded their first corner of the match there was mayhem in their dugout and among their players on the pitch, who were shouting across for instructions. Lorenzo Amoruso was running around his penalty area looking at the backs of the St Johnstone players' shirts to try to see who he should be marking, and Advocaat's assistant, Bert van Lingen, was shuffling bits of paper on which all their tactical notes had been made based on squad numbers. Dick finally realised what had happened and shouted across to me, "You must stop the game! This is not right!" It was absolutely hilarious and for the next ten minutes the two of them were out at the edge of the dugout passing on their hastily rearranged tactics.

On a later occasion I was in charge of a big game at Ibrox and I'd gone into the Rangers dressing room beforehand to check the boots and do my usual pre-match chat. I got my notebook out and went across to him and said, "Right Mr Advocaat, can you just let me know in advance when I'm going to have to come across and give you a telling-off today? That would save us a bit of time." Van Lingen was killing himself laughing, but Advocaat replied, "You have to realise that when I'm shouting at you, it's nothing personal. It's all for my players and our fans. I'm always in control, I always know what I'm doing and why." I knew some managers liked to put on a show for effect down in the dugout, but that was the first time one of them had actually admitted it to me.

The other time that always sticks with me was the first match I'd done after he had taken over at Rangers. It was up at Pittodrie, and for the first fifteen minutes he was going crazy in the technical area, shouting and bawling, waving his arms around, and generally making a nuisance of himself. Eventually I stopped the game and wandered over to him to give him what for, but he stepped on to the pitch towards me, which I'd never seen a manager do previously, and I'm preparing myself for a major confrontation. Instead, he leaned in and said, "Willie, you're having an excellent game." I was completely taken aback and could only reply, "I came across here to say something to you, but now I can't remember what it was!" He was a very clever guy at times.

TERRY BUTCHER (ex-Inverness Caledonian Thistle manager)
It was May 2011 and we were beating Celtic 3–1 late in the second half. As you might imagine, they were laying siege on our goal, bombarding us, as they tried to get back into the match, and we were defending desperately. I knew I needed to break the play up, to try to give our guys a breather, so I decided to make a change and take off our striker Shane Sutherland, who'd scored the third goal. We got Eric Odhiambo ready to go on, and I told Steve Marsella to give the details to the fourth official. He passed over the numbers and the official put up his board showing seven was going on and twenty-eight coming off. There was a bit of confusion, the players were looking around the pitch, and the referee was getting a bit agitated, as were the Celtic coaching staff in the other dugout who were desperate to get the game going again. Eventually everyone realised there wasn't a number twenty-eight out there and that Shane's number was twenty, so the fourth official changed it as quickly as he could, and the switch finally went ahead. The official was having a right go at Steve, who was full of apologies, accepting the blame entirely, and then he gets back into the dugout beside me and gives me a wink. He'd done it deliberately to eat up more time, and it worked, it must have wasted a good thirty seconds, and we went on to win the game 3–2.

STEVEN THOMPSON (ex-Burnley)

It was summer 2009 and we were on a pre-season tour of the USA. The second of the matches was against Portland Timbers, a game we won on penalties after a 2–2 draw, and I scored our second with my first touch of the ball after coming on to replace Steven Fletcher. It was a bizarre set-up in the stadium, as along the front of the stand at pitch level there was an open bar with tables and stools, and a number of the fans sat watching on from there. On top of that, Portland's mascot spent the whole game going round the stadium with a chainsaw, and every now and then he would stop and rev it up to get the supporters cheering. I'd been on the bench for the first hour or so, and it was quite distracting hearing this mascot firing up his machine, and it wasn't much better once I got on the park as I could still hear it buzzing away. It really was quite surreal.

Anyway, as the game moved on I went to close down one of their players, turned to chase after the ball, and lost control. I got a nudge, and that was enough to send me careering off the pitch and past the dugouts. I stumbled over the billboard which ran alongside the track, had to jump to try to stop myself from falling over, and found myself right at one of the tables in the bar. The fans got a bit of a shock and stepped back, and instinctively I reached out, picked up a guy's pint and took a big drink of it before handing it back to him and running back out on to the pitch. The manager, Owen Coyle, said he'd seen plenty players having a drink during his career, but that was the first time it had happened during a game! After the match I went back over to find the guy whose pint I'd shared, I actually wanted to apologise as I hadn't had the chance to speak to him, but he was brilliant about it, thought it had been a great laugh, and I gave my boots to his son as a memento. I know there were reports afterwards that Owen had fined me a week's wages, but he'd just said that tongue-in-cheek when doing his post-match interviews and the American journalists must have taken him seriously.

SCOTT BOOTH (ex-Aberdeen)

Season 1990–91 was my first as a Dons regular. I played in more than twenty matches, started about half of those, but it was a campaign that was to finish with one of the most disappointing days in the club's history, and a real personal sadness for me. We'd been trailing Rangers by a distance in the league, but had put together a brilliant run. We'd won seven games in a row, the last of those a vital 2–1 win over St Johnstone in which we'd come from behind and I'd scored the winner, and at the same time Rangers had been thrashed 3–0 by Motherwell. That meant we went into the final match unbeaten in twelve, and while our goal difference was identical, we had the advantage of having scored more than Rangers. As fate would have it, the last game of the season was a head-to-head at Ibrox, and after those results all we needed was a draw to take the title.

When you look back, that maybe counted against us, as it perhaps put some uncertainty in the minds of the management team, Alex Smith and Jocky Scott. From recollection, we'd played a 4–3–3 formation throughout that incredible run, and it had clearly worked, but for that final match they changed it to a 4–4–2, or that was certainly how it seemed to me, as I was dropped and the midfielder Peter van de Ven drafted into the side. I'd fully expected to start, and only learned I'd be on the bench when the team was read out in the meeting room at our hotel in East Kilbride shortly before departing for the ground. That coach journey was torture. I vividly remember driving through Glasgow, through the hordes of Rangers fans, and the song 'Pump Up The Jam' was playing in the bus, and to this day I can't stand it – when I hear it I have to switch the radio off.

There was construction work going on at Ibrox, so we had to get changed in Portakabins, and you could hear the noise building outside. I was gutted, couldn't believe I'd been dropped for such an important game. Up until that point everything in my career had been on an upwards curve, that was the first serious disappointment I'd had to handle, and I wasn't coping very well. I'm sat down there in the dugout watching the early stages of the match and the overriding memory I have is that it was the loudest stadium I experienced in my whole career. You have to credit the Rangers fans that day, they really turned up for their team, and the noise they generated was so intense. They say that if you have headphones on and turn the volume up really loud it can affect your balance, make you feel disorientated; that's how I felt inside Ibrox that afternoon. It really was incredible, and it got louder when they scored the opener shortly before half-time. It was horrible just sitting in the dugout listening to them celebrate as our title hopes faded away.

I got on after the break, and desperate to make an impact, I picked the ball up wide, cut in, and tried to pass to a teammate, but they intercepted it, broke away, and scored their second. That was it, game over, season over, and after the heartbreak of being left out, I now had that horrible guilt of having been at fault for their deciding goal. You never wanted to be on the bench ever, but that day was one of, if not the worst, of my professional career. I never did ask Alex or Jocky about why they changed the team, why I was left out, but I will one day.

BILLY BROWN (ex-Hearts assistant manager)
It was early in the 2013–14 season and we've got a team of kids playing against Aberdeen. We knew we had a long hard struggle ahead because of the financial problems and the points deduction, and it was vital to get some positive results. It's 1–1, we're down to ten men, but with a couple of minutes left we get a free kick just inside their half and Gary Locke and I are out urging the players forward, and for the ball to be played deep into the box. Callum Tapping hits a great ball and Jordan McGhee outjumps Nicky Weaver to head it into the net. I was already right at the edge of our dugout, and when the ball goes in I'm off celebrating and I'm right in front of the Aberdeen one. Derek McInnes was

145

naturally upset, so he grabs me by the lapels and drags me away, and a scuffle breaks out. It really was an unsavoury scene, and I'm not proud of it.

We're sent away of course, and it carried on all the way up the tunnel, and eventually I get locked in the physio's room to calm down. I was raging, absolutely blazing, but if the roles had been reversed I'd have done the same as Derek. It was back to Hampden for another disciplinary hearing and incredibly we got off with it, a two-match suspended sentence each. I pleaded insanity, I've no idea what Derek said. I couldn't believe it! It was however the same day as the Ian Black case (the Rangers midfielder was banned and fined for breaching SFA rules on gambling) and I think by the end of the day the committee was so fed up they just wanted us out of there.

DEREK McINNES (Aberdeen manager)

Billy is, I don't mind saying, very irritating during the ninety minutes. He moans about everything, he challenges everything – as is his right – but it was the way he celebrated that day, ran into our technical area and gave it the big one right in front of us. I manhandled him back into his own dugout. I was raging, but it's all about getting caught up in the moment, and you do generally regret it afterwards. Billy can be a very nice guy when you meet him out and about, but in the dugout it's very different. We all want to win, and it does boil over, but when it comes to a match-day situation I'd say Billy is as annoying as they come!

I generally know how far I can push it, but that was one of the three occasions I've been sent to the stand during my managerial career. The other two were when I was St Johnstone manager. One was at Tannadice, it was a row over a substitution I was trying to make, and the other was on the final afternoon of the 2009–10 season against Hamilton. It was a tight game going into stoppage time and the ball runs towards the Accies dugout where Billy Reid just steps aside and lets it roll on to waste time.

The match meant nothing, our league position wasn't going to change, but I lost it and went charging into their dugout to get the ball and give it to Dave MacKay to take the throw-in. The fourth official, George Salmond, came across and told me I couldn't enter the opposition technical area and I swore at him, really swore at him. It was only when I was up at Hampden for the disciplinary hearing and I saw what I'd said written down, that I realised just how disrespectful I'd been. I had apologised at the time, but that really brought it home.

CAMPBELL MONEY (ex-Ayr United manager)
It was the 2003–04 season and we were in a tight three-way battle with Raith Rovers and Brechin City to avoid relegation from the First Division. We were playing Brechin away at the start of April, and it was obviously a really important game. I'd left early, before the team, and as I'm driving up the rain was incredible, from Dundee to Brechin it was coming down in horizontal sheets, and I'm thinking there's no way this match is going to be on. I arrive at the ground about 1.15pm, and without being disrespectful, Glebe Park doesn't have the best drainage system in the world so there are puddles all over it. I decided to get changed anyway, and waited for the team to arrive. I spoke to the players, they took a look outside, and the general agreement was there's no chance of it going ahead. Willie Young was the referee and we're all waiting for him to arrive. Two pm comes and there's still no sign of him, but eventually about quarter of an hour later, I see him coming through the front door. I go to speak to him, but he shoots straight into the referee's room, so I wait a few minutes, then knock on the door.

Willie and I go way back, I used to play against him in the Ayrshire amateur leagues when I was with Dailly Amateurs and he played for Vale of Girvan, so we know each other well, and he was very welcoming as ever. I asked if I could have a word, and he said, "What about, Campbell?" I tell him that I'm concerned about the puddles on the pitch, and that I was wondering whether he might postpone the match. "Campbell," he says, "I've been refereeing for nearly twenty years now and I've never yet seen a player drown on a football pitch." So that's game on? "Aye. Game on." It's 0–0 at half-time, and it's not been easy out there, but we score three quick goals soon after the break and we're cruising to what would be a vital win for us given the circumstances. With about ten minutes to go Willie halts the game, picks up the ball, tries bouncing it a few times, has a look around and wanders across to the linesman on the main stand side, Keith Sorbie. I'm standing in the dugout watching this, and bearing in mind this is a relegation battle, I'm going totally apoplectic at the prospect that he might be about to abandon it with us winning 3–0. Anyway, he saunters back across the pitch, has another look around, restarts the game, and we see it out.

At the end I shake hands with the Brechin manager, Dick Campbell, then I stand and wait for Willie to leave the pitch. I reach out to shake his hand and he says, "Congratulations Campbell, big win for you." Then he pauses, smiles, and adds, "I didn't half have you going for a minute there, eh?" before disappearing up the tunnel. I spoke to Keith afterwards and asked him what had gone on during their conversation, and he told me Willie had said, "I'm just having a wee laugh at Campbell's expense. While I'm talking to you, have a look up at the dugout and tell me what his face looks like." That was so typical of Willie, especially later in his career when he would use his sense of humour to handle all sorts of situations. During that time, he was the best ref in the country, but I could have throttled him that afternoon!

ALEX TOTTEN (ex-St Johnstone manager)
There were five minutes left in the game, we're trailing 2–1, and I'm going crazy down in the technical area, trying everything I can to save the match. Everyone who knows me knows I love my golf, I play every Sunday at Glenbervie, and suddenly this

head pops round the side of the dugout, it's one of my pals, and he says, "8.30 tee off tomorrow Totts, don't be late." I couldn't believe it, I'm trying to concentrate, trying to keep my job, trying to get a result, and all he's bothered about is me being on time for the golf the next day.

BILLY STARK (ex-Scotland under-21 coach)

It can be a lonely job down there in the dugout, particularly if the game is going against you. One of my worst ever nights came in August 2013 against England at Bramall Lane. It was a total disaster even down to taking the game, and sometimes circumstances conspire against you.

They had some team with the likes of John Stones, Connor Wickham, Nathan Redmond and Raheem Sterling; Ross Barkley and Harry Kane came on as subs, and to make it worse Roy Hodgson was taking the team, so they all had that extra incentive to impress the national manager. We met on the Sunday, Hibs and Hearts had a TV game so we don't get their players until that night, we take the bus down after they arrive, train once at the ground on the Monday and play on the Tuesday. Our preparation was crap whereas they'd spent a few days at the FA's national centre at St George's Park, and in fact a few of their training sessions were on the FA website and it was pretty frightening watching the quality they had.

I've prepared the boys the best I can, I've warned the back four about ball-watching, and within three minutes the wee boy Redmond gets in behind Clark Robertson and it's 1–0. We do okay without threatening, but they score again just before half-time and our big keeper Jordan Archer miskicks soon after the break to gift them a third. Before I knew it, it was six, and that was one time I had to be out there at the edge of the technical area trying to encourage the lads, letting them know I was with them. I looked up at the clock, and there was still half an hour to go! You talk about feeling lonely, feeling isolated as a manager down there. At that point I'm thinking, 'Bloody hell, can I dig a tunnel here?'

I looked back at the match the next day, and to be honest, that last half hour was just a blur, I'm really not sure how we got through it because they never really let up, they still kept coming at us. The memory of that night will live with me forever. It was a horrible, horrible experience.

BILLY DODDS (ex-Dundee United assistant manager)

We had a Scottish Cup tie with Aberdeen at Tannadice early in 2006. It's always a massive fixture of course, but this one was a real pressure cooker as there had been reports that whichever manager lost would be getting the sack, so the stakes were even higher than normal. We were 2–0 up and giving them a real doing and they go 2–4–4 and we're breaking on them constantly. Collin Samuel has a clear chance – I'll honestly never forget this until the day I die – he was a yard out, all he had to do was put it in the net, but he turned his head and he knocked it a yard wide of the open goal. Typically, they go up the field, big (Derek) Stillie drops the ball and Stevie Crawford scores to get them back into it, he equalises soon after, and then Barry Nicholson goes and wins it with about ten minutes to go. It was such a crushing disappointment, a huge blow, and I was raging.

A couple of months earlier they'd beaten us in a league game at Pittodrie and as I'd been driving home I heard (Aberdeen manager) Jimmy Calderwood on the radio. It had been a tight one, could honestly have gone either way, but Jimmy was on saying how magnificent his team had been, how they could have won by five or six. That made me really angry and I'd been desperate to beat them to ram it up Jimmy. I should have called him before, but didn't, so it had been festering on my mind. At the full-time whistle I shook his hand and congratulated him on the win, but added that he'd been out of order after the previous match. At that, he twisted my finger right back and I fucking exploded. I've gone, there's absolutely no talking to me. Tony Docherty (United coach) and Jimmy Nicholl (Aberdeen assistant manager) are grabbing me, trying to calm me down, but I've lost it completely. I'm trying to kick Jimmy, I'm ripping his shirt, I'm throwing punches at him over the heads of everyone else. Jimmy 'Nic' has just about got me under control when all I hear is Sandy Clark (Aberdeen coach) saying, "Don't worry, I'll sort it out gaffer," and I lose it again.

I'm screaming at Sandy, I'm trying to get to him, trying to kick him now. It was just mental, and it was all my fault, no excuses. I got back to our dressing room, spoke to our boys, then went across to the Aberdeen one, held my hands up and apologised. 'Chis' (United manager Gordon Chisholm) got sacked a few days later, and I was in charge for one game as caretaker manager, and then I was away too. That week was the hardest one of my life, but I won the match against Falkirk, and then I was out. I learned from that afternoon though, and I'd never get involved in that way again. It was incredible, just forty-five seconds of absolute madness. It was frosty for a while with Jimmy after that, but we've had a few pints since and talked about it, and he realised it was all down to the pressure of the moment.

JIMMY CALDERWOOD (ex-Aberdeen manager)
Aye, that was some afternoon, and wee Doddsy's reaction took me completely by surprise. They had been coasting, 2–0 up, and I blew the bugle as I so often did, and threw men forward. It was a great game for us to win and I was obviously delighted at the end. You do have to be conscious of the other manager's emotions though, and I always try to be, but that day feelings were running so high and it all just exploded. As is so often the case, it had all calmed down soon after, and when he told me about the previous game and why my comments had got him so angry, I couldn't believe he hadn't just called me to have it out with me. The job of football manager is hard enough without having those

extra pressures, but when it all kicks off like that it's just because we feel it so passionately, love the game and want to be winners. Taking defeat, especially in those circumstances, isn't easy and the dugout right after the final whistle is just the place for things to get out of hand.

ALEX SMITH (ex-Aberdeen manager)

I've had a number of suspensions and fines, some have been deserved, others less so. One that always annoys me came as a result of a Friday night reserve game at Tannadice. Wee Jim (McLean) loved Friday nights, but I hated them because they disrupted my planning for the first team on the Saturday. Anyway, we'd agreed to this one – I think he'd fixed it up with Jocky (Scott) – and I'm sitting in the directors' box in the corner of the stand, and Jim's there too. The match starts, and it's a donnybrook, tackles flying everywhere, and the young referee is flashing yellow cards. Twenty minutes in we've had three booked, they've had three booked and there's a United player just been sent off. I say to wee Jim that I'm going to try to sort it out, otherwise it's going to be a shambles. I go out the side door and make my way along to the dugout. I call over to the linesman and tell him to have a word with the ref, to ask him to calm down and to just let the players play, let them get on with it. I never raised my voice, I didn't swear or say anything abusive, but the linesman immediately lifts his flag to attract the referee's attention.

Now, the SFA had recently brought in the draconian rule that if that happened, the manager or coach was automatically sent to the stand, and there was an automatic £1,000 fine and a year's ban, so a few weeks later I was up in front of them, and there I was banished again. I'd only just finished the previous suspension! The irony was that I would regularly preach to Jim and to Alex (Ferguson) that if they stayed sitting and shouted abuse from the bench, they'd be all right. In those days, no one was allowed to stand at the edge of the technical area, but if you sat on your backside you could pretty much get away with anything. So there was me, the great lecturer, done for the second time in two years.

To be fair, I could have had no complaints about the other one. We were losing at home to Airdrie in the League Cup, it was late on, and Alex MacDonald's got his players falling down all over the pitch to waste time. Les Mottram was the ref, and Jim Renton was on the line, and I'm screaming across from the dugout to Jim, telling him to get a grip, that Alex was conning them, and he shouts back telling me to shut up. Now, I knew that when the officials were driving up to Aberdeen, they liked to stop in Stonehaven for a cup of tea, so I call back, "See when you stopped for your tea, did you nip into the bookies and get a bet on Airdrie?" Jim was raging, and afterwards I get called into the referee's room and told I'm being reported.

Two of my years in charge of Aberdeen I sat them out in the stand. It was a problem, and it did cause difficulties. The 1990 Scottish Cup Final, late in extra-time, and I think Charlie Nicholas is tiring and I want to take him off and put on Eoin Jess, so I phone down to Jocky and Drew (Jarvie) to tell them. I see them having a chat in the dugout, and Jocky calls back to say they think we should keep Charlie on because he's a penalty taker, and we're close to the shoot-out. I wasn't happy, I had a bad feeling about it, but because I wasn't down there it was difficult to discuss it properly, and I go with them.

What happened? Of course, Charlie scores the pen that takes it into sudden-death – his last kick of the ball as an Aberdeen player before rejoining Celtic that summer – and it goes on and on, with big Brian Irvine eventually slotting home the winning penalty. At the press conference afterwards they're finished with me and they're questioning big Brian, who's a religious guy and has a deep faith in God. He was asked what had been in his mind as he was making that walk from the halfway line, and he said, "I knew that every step I was taking towards the penalty spot, the big man upstairs was with me. I placed so much value in that, and I knew he would see me through, I knew I would score." So I leaned over and asked, "Brian, what about the 50,000 Celtic supporters who were all praying to the same man?"

MARK McGHEE (ex-Millwall manager)
It's part of football that you're regularly up against your mates and in January 2003 we were drawn to play Southampton down at their place in the FA Cup. Gordon Strachan is my best friend, I'd known him for over twenty years at that time, but obviously I wanted to beat him. Steve Claridge scored for us early in the game and out of respect to the wee man I kept my cool, I didn't go over the top with my celebrations. We were playing well and it looked as if we were going to hold out, while they were trying everything to get back in the match.

Gordon stuck on Kevin Davies late on and in the final minute he gets the equaliser, and suddenly the ginger ninja shoots past me and he's doing a Jose Mourinho along the side of the pitch, sliding along on his knees, celebrating as if he's just won the Champions League. I very nearly kicked him up the backside! I spoke to him afterwards and he didn't even realise he'd done it, he'd just got so caught up in the moment. Typically, they beat us in extra time in the replay and went on eventually to lose to Arsenal in the Final.

GORDON STRACHAN (ex-Southampton manager)
I remember that day well, but the difference is his team scored early in the game, that's the secret. You do not jump about the dugout early in the game, you never go crazy when you do that, because anything can happen later in the match. You only jump about and enjoy yourself when you score in the last couple of minutes. Which we did. So, no apologies from me on that score. He'd have done the same!

STUART McCALL (ex-Bradford City manager)

We were down at Luton, it was about five minutes before half-time, and one of our lads was breaking away with the ball when he got taken out by one of theirs right in front of the dugout. It all kicked off, there was a melee, and I ran on to try to separate the players and calm them down, I was pulling the guys apart, settling our lads down, and eventually calm was restored. The referee thanked me for my help, then asked me to leave the pitch, but in the wake of the ruckus he'd lost the plot, had forgotten what had sparked things off, and had awarded them the free kick. I'm screaming from the technical area, telling him he's got it all wrong, but he can't hear me, and of course they go and score from the ball played into our box. That's me, I've lost it, can't believe what's just happened, and I've gone marching back on to the pitch to confront the ref.

The fourth official, who was just a kid, is trying to stop me, but I'm having none of it and I'm shouting at the referee who, quite understandably, sends me to the stand. Now, Kenilworth Road is a strange set-up. The main stand is across from the dugouts, so on the side I'm on there's just a couple of rows of seats and behind them the hospitality boxes. They're all full, and I'm wondering where on earth I'm going to go, when I see some space further down the touchline. I go sprinting along, and still pumped full of adrenalin after what's happened, I easily pull myself up the wall – which is well above head height – and jump over. It's actually a better spot, I'm right above the linesman, so I'm able to keep giving him pelters, and I'm able to shout across to our defenders and goalie, passing on instructions.

Half-time comes, I've been in doing my team-talk, and as we leave the dressing room the fourth official comes up and tells me I'm not allowed to sit back where I was. I have a think about this, I certainly don't want to be over in the main stand, so I decide to wait a few minutes and then sneak back round the other side. I'm creeping round behind the goal and the Bradford fans see me and start chanting my name, so I'm going "Ssssshhh, I don't want to be spotted." Thankfully the play was up the other end, so I get round, place my hands on top of the wall and go to pull myself up. The trouble is I'm all calm now, adrenalined-out if you like, and I can't get up, I'm dangling there like a wee kid, my legs kicking frantically. I realise I can't just stand there, and I can't walk back round as that would be really embarrassing, so on about the fourth attempt I finally manage to scramble up having badly scraped my knees and elbows, roll over the top of the wall, and lie there on the floor for about a minute gasping for air and trying to get my breath back. I try to remain a bit less conspicuous for the rest of the game, and we score in the last minute to force a 2–2 draw.

Of course, I'm down to London a few weeks later for the disciplinary hearing, and they're talking about a £500 fine and a ban for a few matches, but the officials have got their story wrong, they've accused me of swearing at them, which I never did, and my appeal is successful, or at least partly. They never suspended me at all, but they did increase the fine, so I've got to phone my wife after and tell her there's good news and bad news; no touchline ban, which I'm delighted with, but the fine is now £1,000. She wasn't best pleased!

SCOTT BOOTH (ex-Borussia Dortmund)
We were playing Galatasaray in the Champions League and had already run the gauntlet at the airport, the typical Turkish welcome with the 'WELCOME TO HELL' banners, and had our coach windows pelted with bricks and stones on the way to the ground. A few windows had been broken and it was a really uncomfortable journey.

The night of the match, we got changed in the dressing room and went to head out for the warm-up, but found our way blocked by a mass of policemen rigged out in full riot gear. The tunnel is at one end of the stadium and you have to walk up a set of stairs and out on to the pitch, but it's right in front of the hardcore element of the Galatasaray support, and they weren't for taking any prisoners that night. The police held us on the stairs, they've got their heavy-duty riot shields above their heads forming a kind of umbrella, and then they shouted, "Go! Go! Go!" and we darted out on to the pitch. It was only once we were out there and looked back that we fully understood what had happened. The grass was covered with fence poles, metal bars and other serious ammunition, and the police had obviously been waiting for the fans to reload before allowing us out there. I was absolutely terrified, had never experienced an atmosphere quite as intimidating and frightening as that.

I'm on the bench, and for once I'm more than happy with that. It was fine going out to warm up during the game as the dugouts were near the quieter section of the home fans, but you were always looking over your shoulder when you were on the track. The game goes on, it's still 0–0, and the supporters are getting more and more restless. There's about fifteen minutes to go, and I'm sitting in the dugout thinking, 'just let me get out of here in one piece,' when Stephane Chapuisat goes and scores for us, and I'm going, "Oh no! What have you done?" The place goes absolutely mental! We see it out, win 1–0, and then we have to make the reverse journey through that tunnel of riot shields and back to the dressing room as a hail of missiles rained down on us. Even there we weren't safe as there was a window at ground level, and although it was reinforced and had a metal grille covering it, the fans were kicking and punching it, throwing things at it, issuing dire threats towards us. The police kept us in there for a good hour-and-a-half before rushing us on to the bus and away. I can tell you, I have never felt such fear, never been as relieved to leave a stadium and get back to the airport, as I was that night.

JOHN McMASTER (ex-Aberdeen)

We're over in Germany for pre-season training and it's been really tough, a nightmare seventeen days, and Alex Ferguson and Archie Knox have really been working us hard. We finished it off with a round-robin tournament, played a couple of German amateur teams, and then a Romanian side in the final. It's roasting, must have been eighty to ninety degrees and we're knackered after all this. Half-time we're losing 3–1 and Fergie slaughtered us, then sent us back out making it crystal clear he expected an improvement in the second half. Early on they score again and I turn to the bench and I see Fergie wave his hand towards the pitch, and then he and Knox just walk away. He'd had enough, couldn't believe how bad we were, so he decided just to leave us to it and the pair of them went off and had a beer.

DEREK FERGUSON (ex-Rangers)

I was just fifteen, I'd been doing well in the youth team, and the manager John Greig took me aside and told me he was including me in the squad for Tom Forsyth's testimonial match against Swansea, and that I might get the chance to play. I'd done some training with the first team, but I was in awe that day looking around the dressing room at the likes of Davie Cooper, Bobby Russell and Peter McCloy. Big Tam kicked off the game and then came and sat beside me in the dugout. I was nervous, all my pals were in the stands, and I'm sitting there not quite believing it all. I turned to speak to the big man and there he was, relaxing back in his seat puffing away on a cigarette, laughing and joking. I couldn't believe it, had to do a double take. Here was me thinking these legends were all athletes, didn't drink or smoke, trained hard, and here's Tam with his fag. I began to think maybe I should take up smoking, maybe that's how it was done? It was quite bizarre, him sitting there puffing away in the dugout – I'd never seen anything like it. Anyway, I got on for the last twenty-five minutes, made my Rangers debut, and never did have a cigarette along the way.

JIMMY CALDERWOOD (ex-Aberdeen manager)

We had a big game one night, a televised match against Hibs, and I was in the dressing room talking to the players beforehand when Jimmy Nicholl (assistant manager) came in killing himself laughing. I asked what it was all about, but he wouldn't tell me, just said I had to go to the referee's room. I told him I was busy with the lads, but he insisted, so I nipped down the corridor, knocked on the door, and opened it. The linesmen and the fourth official are all sitting there, and they smile at me, but there's no sign of the referee, Craig Thomson. I look at them quizzically and they point over to behind the door, so I pop my head round and there's Craig putting on spray-tan! Now, as everyone knows, I do like the sun, do like topping up my tan, but I burst out laughing and he said, "I was just getting jealous of you Jimmy, so I thought I'd try to match your colour."

PAT BONNER (ex-Republic of Ireland goalkeeping coach)

I was at the 2002 World Cup finals in Japan and South Korea as part of Mick McCarthy's coaching staff, and we did well, making it out of the group thanks to Robbie Keane's late equaliser against Germany and a win over Saudi Arabia in the final match. That meant a knock-out game against Spain, and though we went behind early on, and Ian Harte missed a penalty, Robbie finally scored an equaliser with a second penalty right at the end of the ninety minutes.

It was incredibly hot, really energy-sapping, and by half-time in extra-time, with the score still at 1–1, all our focus was on making sure the players were okay, trying to prevent cramp, working on injuries and geeing them up for one last push in the remaining fifteen minutes. Both of us had made all three substitutions long before then, but unknown to us, one of their subs, David Albelda, had suffered a groin injury and he couldn't continue, so they were down to ten men. It might seem hard to believe, but none of us noticed! I suppose all we were thinking about was our own guys, getting them ready for the rest of the game. At that point it wasn't about the tactical side of things, it was about working on the mental and physical aspects that would be so important, but I do wonder if it might have made a difference had we known. It's no slight on Mick, he was excellent, rather it's a criticism of the rest of us I suppose; you'd have thought one of us might have picked up on it.

Eventually we got word in the dugout about our one-man advantage, but by then it was too late. Would it have mattered had we known sooner? Possibly not, but that was a lesson learnt to always be vigilant in the technical area, and be prepared for anything and everything. In the end we went out on penalties, but it had been quite a performance we'd put up, and that 'what if?' will always stick with me.

ALEX McLEISH (ex-Rangers manager)

It was the final day of the season in 2003, the first of the Helicopter Sundays that we battled out with Celtic. They were down at Kilmarnock and we were at home to Dunfermline and we had the same points, the same goal difference, but we had the slight advantage of having scored one more than them going into those last ninety minutes. I know some of my backroom staff were wanting to know what was happening at Rugby Park, but I didn't. I knew we couldn't control that, all we could do was our own job and go out there and win the match while trying to score as many goals as we could. That's one of the biggest and most important factors of being in the dugout; keeping as clear-headed as possible, staying in control, concentrating on the matter in hand.

Chick Young was the BBC's pitchside reporter that day and he was stationed in behind our dugout, and he kept shouting to me, "Alex, Alex! Celtic have scored." or "Alex, Alex! Kilmarnock have had a penalty claim turned down." Eventually I turned to him and said, "Chick, I don't want to know. Shut the fuck up!

Can you not go and sit twenty rows back, away from me?" To be fair, I had an idea what was happening down the road because of the reaction of the Rangers fans. At one point there was a massive roar went up around the stadium and Barry Ferguson's shouting across to me, asking what's happened, and I'm at the edge of the dugout yelling back that I don't know, but that he should just keep focused on our game. I think everyone assumed Killie had scored then, but it was actually that Celtic had missed a penalty. It was a nerve-wracking day, certainly one of the tensest I've ever experienced in the technical area, but we got there in the end and won the title by the narrowest of margins, just one goal.

JIMMY CALDERWOOD (ex-Dunfermline manager)
What an afternoon that was! There was mayhem going on every-where all around us, but I clearly remember Chick getting very animated behind the dugouts, shouting out to let us know what was happening down the road. At one point he called over that Celtic had been awarded a penalty, and then he went, "They've missed it!" Now, we all know Chick is really a St Mirren fan, but he did seem very happy that afternoon. Very happy!

BILLY BROWN (ex-Hearts assistant manager)
The Edinburgh derby was always a fraught occasion for me, especially when it was at Easter Road. There was a game back in 1997 and I see the ball running towards me in the dugout. I look up and I see 'Robbo' (John Robertson) is in a great position, and I'm thinking if we can take this throw-in quickly, we'll be in with a chance. So, I'm following the ball, but it starts spinning and by the time it crosses the touchline and I pick it up, I'm in the Hibs technical area and Jackie McNamara senior, who was Jim Duffy's assistant, doesn't take kindly to me being there. He grabs the ball and pushes me, and next thing I'm lying in the Hibs dugout and Jim Jefferies, Peter Houston and Paul Hegarty are looking across from ours in astonishment and killing themselves

laughing. Obviously I was well out of order, and the ref Hugh Dallas comes across and I'm expecting to be sent to the stand, but all he did was have a word and told me to get back to my own side. So, I'm up in front of the beaks at Hampden and Hugh is asked why he didn't send me packing, and he replies, "I considered Billy to be one of the less excitable characters in either dugout and thought it best to leave him there." That completely stunned me; given how I react down there I was amazed, but he certainly went up in my estimation that day.

PETER HOUSTON (ex-Hearts coach)

That was one of the funniest things I've ever seen at a game. I had no idea what Billy was up to, hadn't seen the beginning of it, all I saw was Billy sprawled in their dugout. Next thing, Jackie McNamara is pushing him, John Ritchie (Hibs coach) is pulling him, they're chucking him back and fore between them, they're rag-dolling him, and Billy's going absolutely nuts, shouting and screaming. I couldn't believe it when he was allowed to return back to our technical area!

CHAPTER NINE

PAT NEVIN

Pat Nevin was the type of footballer Scottish fans love to watch, a throwback to the great 'wee wingers' that have carved glowing reputations in the history of the game. From the early days of football to the 1928 'Wembley Wizards', through the war years, and well into the 1960s, those were the players who thrilled supporters. The names will be well remembered by older fans: Alex Jackson, Alan Morton, Davie Wilson, Jimmy Johnstone and Willie Henderson. There was Willie Johnston and Alex Edwards, Tommy McLean, and a little more recently the likes of Gordon Strachan and John Robertson.

As football changed, both in terms of style and tactics, there was, for a time, less emphasis placed on such mercurial talents, managers instead opting for taller, stronger, more physical athletes. It meant the smaller kids had to work even harder to get noticed, to make the breakthrough, and Nevin falls firmly into that category.

Rejected by his boyhood heroes, Celtic, for being too light-weight, the Glaswegian signed instead for Clyde, then in the bottom tier of Scottish football, and set about trying to prove the doubters wrong.

He did that in spectacular fashion, helping them to win the title, and promotion, in his first season. Within two years he had earned a move to Chelsea as part of John Neal's reconstructed side, and as the club's Player of the Year was instrumental in guiding the Stamford Bridge club back to the top flight of the English game.

After five successful years he was sold to Everton for almost £1 million, and while he continued to make an impact at Goodison, he was – as will be outlined later – eventually forced out by his manager, Howard Kendall.

Pat crossed the Mersey to spend five seasons with Tranmere Rovers before returning north of the border, initially with Kilmarnock and then Motherwell where, uniquely, he was for a spell player/chief executive, the latter role one in which he could fully utilise the knowledge gained while studying commerce as a teenager.

He retired from playing in 2000, ending a career in which he had also accumulated twenty-eight international caps for his country and well and truly proved that he wasn't 'too small' to compete in professional football.

For much of his two decades he was a regular first-team starter, so did not spend much time sitting on the bench. The exceptions were a frustrating spell with Everton, large parts of his time away with Scotland, and the very early days with Clyde at the old Shawfield Stadium.

'The first few months of my first season I was going ballistic. I was on the bench every week and I was desperate to show what I could do. I was stuck there in the dugout and it was the physio who wouldn't let me play! The manager, Craig Brown, would turn to him and ask "What do you think?" and the physio, wee John Watson, would say, "Nah, he's not ready yet." It was driving me nuts and so when I was finally let loose I was like a bullet from a gun, I was so eager, and I hit top form right from the start and was hardly out of the team again. It was only years later, when I was more experienced, that I realised they had just been playing me, it was all part of their dugout routine, a way of ensuring that when I got the chance I would make sure I took it.

'When I moved to Chelsea I went into the first team within weeks, so had little experience of life in the technical area at club level, but I got plenty of it with the international side.

'When you're with the national squad it's weird, really strange in the dugout, because what you have is a bunch of guys who are not used to being on the bench, so you've almost got a bad vibe already. There'd be boys there with grumpy faces, sitting with their arms crossed. Look at any dugout and you'll almost always see them. There'll be a few jumping about, encouraging their teammates on the park, but you'll also have those who'd rather be anywhere else than among the subs. Someone misses a chance, or comes close to scoring, and most of the subs are up going 'No!' or their arms are up in the air, but there might be two guys sitting there just chatting away to each other and not really bothering.

'There's an argument that such an attitude should be expected, you should always feel you're good enough to be playing. I certainly felt that way, but I decided I wasn't going to go dragging everyone around me down by mumping and moaning about it.

'You'd be sitting beside the guy who's a star with his team and he's pissed off, everyone is to an extent I suppose, and you could sense that vibe a lot of the time. They all want to be playing. It always seemed to me that the Anglos (Scottish players with English clubs) were angrier, but I made a point to be chipper, happy, and as often as I could, never in the dugout. I would always be out there warming up. Over my ten years I must have been in around one hundred squads, but I only ever made it on to the park on twenty-eight occasions, and if you look back at the footage, you'll see me out on the track, or behind the goal, but rarely sat on the bench. I just saw that as a complete waste of time, and I always preferred to be out preparing for the call to action, whenever it came.

'You weren't supposed to do it, but I'd hide a ball inside my top then head down to the end of Hampden and what I'd do was practise my skills the whole time. What that meant was that if I got the shout with ten minutes left in the game, I'm ready, I didn't need to then start warming up. I had my touch, my feel for the ball, I could go on right away.

'It was something I put a lot of thought into, mainly because I'd spent so little time in the dugout with my club. I just wanted to make sure that whenever called upon, I could go out there and give my best for my country.

'I do recall one time I was sitting on the bench alongside my mate Brian McClair and the manager, Andy Roxburgh, turned and looked at the two of us, clearly trying to decide which to put on. He picked 'Choccy', who sprang from his seat and whipped off his tracksuit bottoms, and there he is standing in the Hampden dugout with no shorts on, just his jockstrap. I'm going "put me on, put me on instead" but Andy decided to delay the substitution, let McClair go back to the dressing room and find a pair of shorts, and then put him on. I'm not sure what that said about me!

'Andy and Craig Brown worked very hard on fostering a real team spirit within the Scotland squad, on getting the right attitude in training, on the pitch, around the hotels we stayed in, and that definitely extended to the technical area during matches. They were meticulous in everything they did.

'I mentioned that 'bad vibe', well as time moved on that changed. 'Roxy' really worked on that, and in the later part of my Scotland career we were a group together, and it meant that everyone in that dugout was jumping up and down when we scored. He'd got rid of that 'what am I doing here, wasting my time' attitude that had been prevalent in the past, and it made a huge difference, completely changed the atmosphere within the technical area.

'I suppose what helped was the natural evolution within the

squad. As the older players dropped out you had the younger guys like me, Paul McStay, McClair and Bryan Gunn coming in, and we were more open to the manager, delighted to be part of the set-up, and more prepared to sit on the bench and wait our time. Craig and Andy did so much to encourage good ethics and that positive spirit in the dugout was an important part of the overall picture.

'Eventually, if anyone was behaving badly, we self-policed it and had a go at the individual concerned.

'At any football club, in any squad, you'll find that the strongest characters lead the attitude, the ethos, and for a number of years in the teams I played in, the strongest characters had terrible attitudes, it was all about them and not the group. In the end, we got away from that with Scotland and we were proud to be there, proud to be representing our country. It didn't matter if you were playing or sat on the bench, we had a good positive attitude and did everything we could to maintain that.

'You have to remember I'm Chelsea's player of the year, 'Choccy' has just scored over twenty league goals in a season for Manchester United – the first player to do so for the club since George Best a couple of decades earlier – and yet time after time we were left out, often because a few Celtic or Rangers players suddenly decided they were fit and available for certain games. But we never grumbled about it, we just got on with it and played what part we were asked to.

'That said, my attitude was always, "I want on now, I want on now" and while I wouldn't warm up right in the manager's face, I would always try to make sure he could see I was ready, that I was buzzing, that I was physically up for it. I figured that if it's a toss-up and the manager can't decide who to put on, if one guy is sitting in the back row with his feet up and another is going through all his warm-up routines, he's going to choose the latter.

'There was one bitterly cold, rainy night at Hampden and I was warming-up with trainers on. Andy spotted this and asked, "Are you ready to go on?" and I said I was. He pointed at the trainers and I explained it was all part of my process. I'd been dribbling, working on my skills as I did, getting my feel and touch, essentially warming my feet up. All the rest of the guys are sitting there in the dugout, and their feet are freezing, their boots are wet. I slip mine on, my feet are warm and dry, and I'm ready to go. It was entirely calculated on my part; for me, just normal professionalism. Just think, you go on to the pitch and the ball comes to you right away; your feet are like blocks of ice, you can't control it. It makes no sense at all, so I made a point of using trainers whenever the weather was bad.

'I would always study the manager when I was on the bench. I'd try always to be in their eyeline, in their thoughts, but I'd also make sure to listen carefully to what they were saying. You'd hear them crack up at a player, 'What's he doing that for?' and you'd think, right, I won't do that when I get on. I would also study the match, I'm looking at every one of the opposition, especially the full-backs, trying to pick up on any weaknesses. Ah, the right-back, he can't kick with his left foot at all, excellent, I'll remember that if I get put on. He tends to dive in, great, that's registered, I'll watch out for that.

'I've figured out that if I get on to the pitch I'll probably get half a dozen touches. Six times I'll have the ball at my feet, so I can't afford to waste any of them.

'The perfect example of that was a Euro 92 qualifier against San Marino when it was 0–0 after about an hour. Everyone's getting more and more frustrated, more and more angry, and I'm sitting on the bench and I'm thinking, 'I know the answer, put me on.' They were packing the box, they were lunging into tackles, and all you needed to do was run at one of them with pace, flick it round them, and they would take you out. Eventually I catch Andy's eye and he puts me on for 'Choccy' and within a couple of minutes I've won us a penalty. I'd targeted the one guy I wanted to go at because he was the rashest of them all, so I ran towards him in the box, dummied, then moved the ball away, and his feet weren't as quick as mine. Have a look at the video, it's very clear that I know exactly what I'm doing, I flick the ball and he brings me down. Penalty, Gordon Strachan scores it, we go on to win 2–0. That was all very calculated and I was able to do it because while I'm sitting there in the dugout, I'm paying attention to the game. It's just common sense.

'I've always said if I'm told I'm getting one half of a game, give me the second half. For a start, the opposition are more tired, there's more space, and most importantly of all, you've had a chance to watch them in action, to study them, to identify any flaws and weak points you can capitalise on.

'That approach extended beyond the technical area for me and as soon as I could, I kept video tapes of every game I played in. It must have been my second season with Chelsea they started filming each match, so I came to an agreement with the manager that I'd get the tape once he'd finished with it. I'd watch them over and over, decide which things worked and which things didn't, and refined my game that way. Once I'd decided which tricks were most effective, I went off and practised them until I'd perfected them, and I continued to do that throughout the rest of my career.

'All of that fed into keeping me on the pitch, and off the bench, as much as possible, but on the occasions I was a substitute, I was determined to go on, make an impact, and make it more likely that I'd get a starting place next time round. It was something of a scientific approach I guess, but it seemed the right way to go about it for me. You go on and score a goal, the manager's going to remember that, isn't he?

'There was of course the fear of being labelled a 'super-sub' and that did haunt me a wee bit with Scotland. I won twenty-eight caps, but only started fifteen of those games, and there's no doubt I was seen by many as more of an impact player coming off the bench. I scored five times, which wasn't bad, but my assists were just as important to me, and I reckon I had about a dozen of them, many after coming on as a substitute. The simple fact was that Andy Roxburgh, then Craig Brown, knew that if we were up against a packed San Marino or Faroese defence, I was the ideal type of player to put on to try to unlock it.

'Away from the international scene I'd had little or no experience of being in the dugout at club level for years, but that all changed when Everton reappointed Howard Kendall as their manager. Right from the start we didn't get on. I didn't like him and he didn't like me, considered me a dangerous individual because I'd once read a book – that was his mentality at the time. I'd been playing really well, perhaps the best football of my career, and he tried to sicken me by continually putting me on the bench.

'Kendall had brought in the Polish player, Robert Warzycha, who played in the same position as me, and he was starting irrespective of how he'd played the previous week. This went on for half a season, and every week I'd warm up in front of the manager, make sure he saw me constantly. I'd do that for eighty-eight or eighty-nine minutes, and then he'd put me on, and it was all about trying to force me out of the club. I was stubborn, kept at it, but I was wrong, I should have left. I wasted a year trying to prove to him that I was a player and he just wasn't interested. That was reinforced after one game against Oldham. I'd gone on late in the match as ever and happened to score the winner, and when we were all back in the dressing-room afterwards, in front of the lads, Kendall said loudly, "Jammy goal that one, eh?" That was it, I knew my time there was over.

'Part of my drive then was that I was trying to get into the Scotland squad for the Euro 92 finals. I knew they wanted to take me, but I had to be playing regularly, and so I bit the bullet and left for Tranmere, initially on a month's loan.

'I got to the finals, then that summer had a choice between signing for Galatasaray or Tranmere, and I chose Rovers – go figure. As luck would have it, our first pre-season friendly was at Prenton Park, against Everton!

'So, I'm up against their full-back, Pat van den Hauwe, and I'm looking to attack him. He showed me inside, then leathered me with real force, and all of a sudden I'm running out of control and heading straight for the dugout. The away dugout. Kendall is sitting down there and sees me coming, and all I see is his eyes widening further and further as I get closer. I go careering over the touchline and he's shrinking back into his seat, and I see the fear in his eyes. The only thing I can do is put out my foot to stop my momentum, and as I reach the very edge of the dugout I push it out, my boot goes whizzing just past his head, and my studs go slamming into the wood; they're embedded there about an inch from his ear. I stood there trying to free my boot and I leaned in and said, "I was sorely tempted." And I was, I could have done him serious damage, but hey, life's too short. As I walked away, he burst out laughing, I think more out of relief than anything else. I'm not a violent guy, but just for a moment then I loved seeing the terror on that man's face.

'As a winger, quite often hogging the touchline, you are the obvious first point of contact for the manager, so you're used to passing on messages to other players, and I would do that, even if some of the instructions seemed quite bizarre at times. I rarely got much in the way of personal orders though, managers seemed to be generally happy to let me play my game, or maybe they just knew I would ignore them!

'The one exception was a new coach, Ernie Walley, who came in towards the end of my time at Chelsea. He was a long-ball man, and he hated seeing me setting off on my dribbling runs. There was one match where we had Kevin McAllister on one wing and me on the other, and I picked the ball up on halfway, beat a couple of players, took it to the bye-line and crossed, and Gordon Durie headed just over. It was a thrilling move, the fans were all up on their feet cheering, but as I ran back up the pitch, Walley shouted across, "I told you, if you take more than two touches you're getting substituted!" I just shook my head and turned to the bench and gave him a mouthful. I left Chelsea that summer.

'I don't ever remember either Andy or Craig giving me personal instructions from the technical area when I was playing with Scotland, but the time when I knew I would be getting the shout from any manager was always when a player, particularly perhaps a goalkeeper, was sent off. You're the closest to the touchline, you're seen maybe as something of a luxury, so as soon as the red card is flashed, you got the hook! That was so infuriating.

'When I returned home and played with Kilmarnock I tended to play rather than sit on the bench, and then of course I moved to Motherwell and became the club's chief executive while continuing my playing career. I was in the dugout more often then, as part of the match-day squad, and also as a place where I could have private conversations during the week with the owner, John Boyle, and the manager, Billy Davies.

'It was something of a strange situation. I'm Billy's boss, but the one thing I can't talk to him about is the game, or his team selection. I can't say 'pick me' because that would be seen as meddling, and if I'm among the substitutes, I can't tell him to put me on. I've appointed him and I've got to let him get on and do the job. Anyway, I think everyone will have long since realised that Billy's not the kind of guy who's going to take advice, he's very much his own man. So, I'd just have to sit on the bench and bite my tongue. I thought I should still be playing, of course I did, but I couldn't say so.

'Across my career there were lots of the standard dugout laughs; guys forgetting to put their shorts on like 'Choccy', guys cracking their heads off the roof, or tripping and falling over during celebrations, all kinds of scenarios which left everyone there taking a fit of the giggles. There were the funny, and not so funny, reactions of players who were being subbed off; there was the excitement, the enthusiasm of players being told they were going on, particularly for Scotland, getting the chance to win another international cap, but one that always sticks with me was big Duncan Ferguson.

'We were on tour in America, a warm-up before Euro 92. I'd scored within the first ten minutes against the US, and we won the game 1–0, but I got injured early in the second half, and my replacement was big Dunc, which clearly meant a change in the tactical approach. I love the big guy, I'd just spent two nights with him, and he's nuts, but he's great, and I'm thinking this is his big chance to force his way into the team for the finals, he's going to go out there and bust a gut, try to really make an impact. So I'm sitting on the bench, and I'm studying him. The first ball goes up towards him and he just stands there, watches it sail over his head. A couple of minutes later, the same thing, and this continues right up to the final whistle. Afterwards, Andy Roxburgh goes round all the players having a chat, and he gets to Dunc. I'm pissing myself laughing, wondering how he's going to approach it. He asks if the big man is okay, and Dunc just waves his hand dismissively and says, "Ach, I can't get myself up for these friendlies, these bloody park games." Of course, Andy's so serious and he quickly tries to move on, but the tears were streaming down my face. It was so funny, Duncan was just on a different planet in those days! He's a fantastically interesting guy now, but back then he was just crazy.

'I had so many laughs during my career, that was an important part of every dressing room I was in, and the fun helped foster the team spirit that is so important there, on the park, and as I've said, in the dugout. I might not have been typical, but I did see those times on the bench as a crucial part of my development, and I tried to use my time well, to study and analyse, to try to find that little something that would give me an edge when I got out on the park, because let's be honest, that's the best part of being a footballer, playing the game, showing your skills and lapping up the response from the fans.'

CHAPTER TEN

TALES AWAY FROM THE DUGOUT

The process of collecting stories for this book was a time-consuming, but hugely rewarding one. There were countless laugh out loud moments as players, managers and referees recalled the bizarre, and at times quite frankly unbelievable, scenarios that seem to play out daily in and around football stadiums and training grounds. Many of these incidents are considered run-of-the-mill by those involved, but for those of us on the outside, not normally privy to such happenings on the pitch, in the dressing room or down in the dugout, they can be real eye-openers.

I was often left speechless while hearing how sane, rational, quietly-spoken guys turn into raving madmen during match-day, with the technical area the prime breeding ground for such lunacy.

Insults are spat out, punches are thrown, as all reason goes out of the window and being awarded that throw-in, or that free kick on the halfway line, becomes the most important thing in the world.

More often than not during our chats, the interviewee would say, "Oh, I've got this great story, but it's not really about the dugout . . ." and while I did try to be disciplined, my natural curiosity as a football fan would get the better of me, and I'd sit back in the chair and revel in it. Usually when they had recalled one such occurrence, another would spring to mind, which meant some of the sit-downs lasted considerably longer than had been arranged. The bottom line is, football people like to talk football, and they love to have a laugh.

The more such stories I was told, the more I realised they simply could not be left out, they had to be shared, and that is why the final chapter is filled with Tales Away From The Dugout.

DEREK McINNES (Aberdeen manager)

We were in the Europa League playing the Dutch side Groningen and there's a strict protocol the night before where the away team gets access to the stadium for training, the press and media are allowed in for the first wee while, then they go, and none of the opposition football staff is allowed to be there. But you're always careful, you wouldn't want to be too detailed in terms of the tactics just in case there's a spy in your midst. Our fitness coach Graham (Kirk) is putting the boys through their warm-up and I happen to glance up at one of the hospitality boxes and I see their manager sitting there watching on. I call over the UEFA delegate to tell him and I point up to the box, and as we look up we see his chair slowly being pushed backwards and him disappearing out of view. The delegate calls over someone from the club and he point-blank denies it, saying the manager is off watching a game, and I say, "Yes, this one." I'm not going to say I've never watched the opposition here at Pittodrie, but I make sure I'm not caught!

At least Groningen tried to cover it up; in the previous round the Latvian side Daugava Riga were entirely blatant about it, they didn't give a shit. Their manager and captain just sat out in the middle of the stand and watched the whole session. We asked them to move and they refused, they didn't budge, and after we'd finished they came up and thanked us and shook our hands.

DAVID VAN ZANTEN (ex-Hibernian)

We had a couple of days off, it was an international weekend, so I thought I'd take my wife for a lovely romantic break at Cameron House Hotel on Loch Lomond. When we arrived, the room wasn't quite ready so we went off to the bar. A while later I went up to check in and thought I'd take a look at the room first. When I got there, there was what looked like an expensive bottle of Champagne sitting on the table and a card which read, 'To my beautiful wife Lyndsay. I love you very much. David'. Now, I'd had a few drinks by this stage and I had to sit down on the bed and have a think – had I organised this? I eventually convinced myself I hadn't, so went back to reception to query it, and the girl told me I'd called earlier and asked not only for their most expensive bottle of Champagne, but for rose petals to be strewn across the bed. She apologised they hadn't been able to organise the flowers at such short notice. It was a bit awkward, but I explained that I had done no such thing, and when the receptionist offered to have the bottle removed I thought, 'My wife doesn't know about this' and said yes, they should do just that. I never mentioned it to Lyndsay for a while, but eventually confessed, and started texting around to try to find out who'd done it. After a while my teammate John Rankin finally called in fits of laughter and admitted it had been him. I never found out how much that bottle would have cost me, but they told me it was the most expensive they had – it would probably have been a whole week's wages!

DEREK ADAMS (ex-Aberdeen)

One day when I was with Aberdeen, we go back in at half-time and things haven't been going well. The boss, Jimmy Calderwood, turns to our striker Noel Whelan and says, "You're not doing it today big guy, I'm going to have to take you off." Noel replies, "You're not taking me off," and Jimmy says, "Yeah, you're coming off." So big Noel just strips off and heads through

177

to the bath. Jimmy Nicholl (assistant manager) leans across to the gaffer and asks who he's putting on instead, and there's a few seconds of silence. "Fuck, I don't know, you'd better go and get Whelan out of the bath." So Nicholl goes through to the bath and says, "Noel, the gaffer's maybe made a wee mistake here, he's had a go at you, a bit of a misjudgment, but he wants you to go back out for the second half." Big Noel refuses, he's lying there relaxed and soaking in the nice warm bath, and Nicholl is pleading with him. Whelan strings him along a bit, refusing point blank to get out, he's soaping himself, he's sliding down in the water rinsing himself off, and Jimmy is getting more and more agitated. Eventually he smiles, gets out, dries off, gets his strip back on, saunters nonchalantly back up the tunnel, and makes it out to rejoin us just in time for the referee to restart the match.

ERIC BLACK (ex-Coventry City assistant manager)

Gary McAllister had taken over at Coventry and I was brought in as his assistant. Because Gary was still playing as well, much of the responsibility in the dugout fell on my shoulders and I was doing a lot of the coaching and the half-time talks, that sort of thing. Because I was so heavily involved, Gary got me a desk in his office and that meant we could discuss and assess things constantly. He was under a bit of pressure to cut costs, so we went through the squad and there were a couple of Honduran players who were on big money, but not good enough to play regularly, and so he decided they had to go. One of them, Jairo Martinez, had been struggling with a knee injury anyway, and he was to be the first to be told, so Gary called him up to the office. He'd thought it all through, knew just what he was going to say, and had planned it out, even down to the fact that he would tell the player that his pay-off would be in US dollars, as the Central American players preferred to talk in that currency.

At the agreed time, Jairo came in and sat down, and Gary

launched into his spiel. I have to say it was very impressive, very convincing. He explained that he was the new manager and that he didn't see Martinez fitting into his plans, he wanted different kinds of players to fit into his vision for how the team would play under him, but that the club would be easy to deal with, and would do what they could to help him move on. He outlined what types he felt he needed, and why the Honduran didn't fit the bill. He explained that a large part of his contract would be paid up, around $200,000, but that if there were any tax implications he and his advisors would have to deal with that. This went on for a good twenty minutes, Gary doing all the talking, and I'm sitting there thinking, 'Well done, you're doing a great job selling this, you've nailed it.'

Eventually Gary stops talking and looks across at Martinez, who smiles warmly, and replies in halting English, "My knee, it is much better now. Thank you gaffer." He hadn't understood a single word the manager had said! We did eventually get him out of the club, but it took a while longer than Gary had hoped.

BILLY STARK (ex-St Mirren)

We were playing Partick Thistle at Love Street, right at the start of the season after we'd been promoted to the Premier Division, and Alex Ferguson and wee Bertie Auld (the Thistle manager) didn't like each other. We won 2–1 and we knew he'd be in a good mood after the game, and he was, for him. You had to measure things differently, he never said 'fantastic, brilliant' but if he said 'well done' you knew you'd done exceptionally well, and he'd been saying that to us in the dressing room. He then disappeared upstairs, but he told our captain, Jackie Copland, to tell us to wait behind, that he wanted to talk to us again. We got showered and changed, and we waited and waited, it must have been near six o'clock and we're all wondering what it's about. Someone points out we've not got our medals yet for winning the First Division, so we think maybe that's it, he's going to be presenting us with them and congratulating us on all our effort and hard work in the previous season.

At that point he bursts into the room, the door nearly comes off its hinges, and he picks up an empty juice bottle from the crate that's sitting there and he throws it across the room. I'm sure he meant it to go through the open toilet door, but he missed, and it smashed on the wall beside and the players sitting under it all got showered with pieces of glass. He's going nuts, he's calling us for everything, going absolutely crazy. It eventually became clear what it was all about. Players from a number of teams, Partick Thistle and ourselves included, used to go into the Waterloo Bar in Glasgow for a few pints on a Saturday evening after games. It was nothing heavy, just a chance to relax with the guys and socialise a bit. He's screaming, "You'll no' be going in there with those Partick has-beens!" and you know, he actually made us all sign a piece of paper promising we wouldn't go into the Waterloo again. He was so controlling, so unpredictable. There we were expecting a pat on the back and our winner's medals, and that's what we got instead.

NEIL SIMPSON (ex-Aberdeen)

We had won the league the previous year but there had been a row over the bonuses paid out, and the players weren't happy, there was dissent in the ranks. To try to smooth things over, Alex Ferguson came into the dressing room ahead of a pre-season match and said that everyone who played that day would get £500. I'm only eighteen and I'm sitting there thinking, 'Oh you beauty! Five hundred quid?' They've obviously bumped it up as a goodwill gesture and I can't believe it, that was a huge sum of money to me back then.

A year later, we're playing Arsenal pre-season and the manager comes in and says, "Right, I've spoken to the chairman and we'll pay you the same bonus as we did last year, that's £300." There's a bit of grumbling around the dressing room and Willie

Miller says he thought it had been £400. Fergie's not happy at this and as he's about to reply I stick up my hand and say, "It was actually five hundred last year."

He completely exploded: "What the fuck do you know about bonuses!" He came right across and screamed at me, there was spit all over my face as he continued the tirade. Then he turned, went flying out the room, and slammed the door behind him. I just sat there, petrified, and the rest of the players all leaned round, looked at me, and shook their heads in disbelief. You know, I never made the first-team squad for about four months after that, that was my punishment. Funnily enough, in later years whenever there was a discussion over bonuses, Fergie would always turn to me and ask, "What do you think Simmy?"

STUART McCALL (ex-Motherwell manager)
I've been up in front of a disciplinary committee twice. The first was when I got let off as Bradford manager, and the second was in March 2012 after a Scottish Cup tie against Aberdeen, and again I escaped a ban. On that occasion they'd wrongly been given an early corner from which they opened the scoring, and they went on to knock us out. At half-time I'm heading down the tunnel and I glance down to my right where the referee's room is, and see the officials disappearing down it. I shout across, "You'll be embarrassed when you see the replay linesman. Embarrassed!"

A few minutes later I'm in our dressing room talking to the players and there's a knock on the door. It's the fourth official and he's telling me the ref, Craig Thomson, wants to see me in his room. I try to explain that I'm doing my team-talk, but he's adamant, and so I march down the corridor and Craig tells me he's sending me to the stand for harassing the match officials. We get the report in a few days later and it claims that I've stood and waited for them, then subjected them to 15 seconds of abuse. It so happens we've got a video camera down there, and when we looked back at the footage it clearly showed that I was just walking through and that the whole thing lasted no more than 2–3 seconds. They didn't have a leg to stand on!

Off we go to Hampden, we show it to Craig, and he goes in and tells the three-man committee that he's got it wrong. I get called in next and they tell me that I've been found not guilty, but only because the referee has told them the truth. Eh, no it's there in black and white, the video evidence, they've seen exactly what happened. I was raging, couldn't believe it, but I kept calm, didn't say a word, and that meant that in all my time as a football coach or manager I've still never been banned from the touchline, which I'm quite proud of.

CAMPBELL MONEY (ex-St Mirren)

We were playing Dundee United at Tannadice, and from memory I think it was around Christmas time. As a goodwill gesture, each player was given a plastic football and the idea was that we would kick them into the crowd before the start of the game. This was all spelled out to us and the two teams lined up in the tunnel behind the referee, Kenny Hope, and his linesmen. He leads us out and across to the halfway line where, as planned, we all wave to the fans, split up, then go across to our own supporters and dispatch the balls as instructed. We turn round and get ready to start play and Kenny is standing looking a bit bewildered. The reason soon became apparent; Ian Ferguson had kicked the match-ball into the crowd, and the lucky recipient wasn't about to own up! We then had to hang around while the United ground-staff tried to locate another suitable ball so we could finally get the game underway.

IAN MAXWELL (ex-St Mirren)

Charlie Adam joined us on loan in the 2005–06 season, and he did well for us. Didn't play every game, but you could see he was a player, and he certainly made something of an impact. Towards the end of the season, John Potter and I went on to the

SPFA (players' union) website, downloaded all their graphics and mocked up a letter telling Charlie he had been nominated for the First Division player of the year award, and posted it into the club. He was thrilled, started telling all his family, in fact he was so delighted I think he was stopping people in the street to tell them! Everyone at the club knew, we even got one of the local newspaper reporters to come in and interview him and he's sitting there saying how proud he is to have been recognised by his fellow pros. He's even told the chairman he'd better get a couple of tables at the dinner so all the players can go along to support him. We'd got him hook, line and sinker and he wasn't best pleased when we not so subtly broke the news to him that it was a wind-up. He was gutted!

We had a lot of fun with Charlie actually. There was another day he came in and he asked 'Hinchy' (goalkeeper Craig Hinchcliffe) to use his hair clippers to trim the back of his neck. So Charlie sits down on the chair in the middle of the dressing room and we're all looking at each other, can't believe he's actually done this. 'Hinchy' agrees, picks up the clippers, and runs them right up the back of his head and across the top. It was like a reverse Mohican! If you look back at pictures from that season you'll see Charlie was sporting a close cropped look for part of it – that was the reason why.

ALASDAIR ROSS (assistant referee)
Inevitably you get asked about the big name players. I've been fortunate enough to do games involving Lionel Messi and Cristiano Ronaldo and I have to say I prefer the Argentine. At Euro 2012 I was doing Portugal's game against Denmark and I was responsible for checking the Portuguese players in the tunnel. I make my way down the line checking their boots and their undershorts and when I get to Ronaldo he takes a step back, holds his palms out in front of himself, and says, "You don't check me, I'm perfect." So there was a bit of a stand-off, and eventually I have to say to him, "Let me see your fucking boots or

you're not going out." So that was before the game even started, and then at half-time I'm counting the Portugal players back out from the dressing room and there's only ten of them. I ask one of the coaches where the eleventh player is and he says, "That'll be Ronaldo, his stylist is still doing his hair for the second half." You watch the game back on video and you'll see right enough he's got a different hairstyle in the second half.

PAT NEVIN (ex-Chelsea)

I'd gone to what was then called Glasgow Technical College as a kid, studied for a BA Commerce, and I've always said that all the subjects I took – Law, Economics, Accounts, Marketing – later came in useful during my football career, but when I was at Chelsea, it was my Statistics which helped me get one over the chairman, Ken Bates. I'd had a really good season, won player of the year, and I'm on buttons, £180 a week. My rent was £100, take tax off my wages and I've got £20 a week to live on in central London. 'Batesy' realised I was worth a bit more, so he calls me into his office and it's like the whole 'CJ – Reggie Perrin' routine, you're sitting down below on a wee chair, and he's towering above you, you can barely see his head above his desk. He told me I was definitely getting a new contract and asked what I wanted. I told him to make me an offer and he said no, it doesn't work like that, that I had to make a demand. I refused to do so, pointing out he'd called me in, he should make the first move. He asked if I had an agent, I said no, and he was getting quite flustered. Eventually he told me to go away and come back the next day and tell him what I wanted.

So I went off, spoke to some of the lads, and typed up a list of my demands. Twenty-four hours later in I go and hand over this A4 sheet detailing £500-a-week wages, a signing-on fee and a number of return flights from London to Glasgow. He lifted it up, looked at it, scrunched it up, chucked it in the bin, stormed out of his office slamming the door behind him, marched straight into his *Rolls Royce Corniche* and he was gone. He never actually said a word. I'm sitting there, a kid of nineteen in this huge office, not sure what to do, and it strikes me; I'm from Easterhouse, I know exactly what I'm going to do here. So I rifle through all his drawers and find the contracts of all the first team players, write down all the amounts, and go home that night and do a 'mean, median and mode' calculation to get the average payments.

Next day, I'm back in the office and he asks if I've had a rethink, and I say, "Yes, I want twenty-five-pounds-a-week more." I thought he was going to explode! He shouted that nobody was on £525 a week, and I replied, "No, nobody's actually on it, but that's the average." He pointed out that I couldn't possibly know that, and I said, "Yes I do, I went through your drawers last night and found all the contracts." There was a silence, he looked me in the eye, and then he burst out laughing and said, "Brilliant! It's yours." We always got on very well after that.

BILLY DODDS (ex-Queen of the South coach)

We trained down at Glasgow Green and they were a great bunch of boys. We worked hard, but had a lot of fun, and there was always one voice louder than all the others; Neil Scally's. He's a loveable rogue Neil, you hear him before you see him, and this particular morning he's making an absolute racket as he comes down the hall to the dressing room. You always know it's him, not just because of the noise, but because he's got a really pronounced lisp, the worst I've ever heard. The previous night there had been a Bayern Munich Champions League game on the telly and Bastian Schweinsteiger had scored an absolutely unbelievable goal, right in the top corner, and I hear 'Scalls' raving about it, so I call him into the office. I'm there along with the manager, Gordon Chisholm, big Kenny Brannigan and the goalkeeping coach, Peter Latchford, and I tell him they hadn't seen it, that he has to describe it to them. He's always so enthusiastic, he's bouncing around in the room, and he starts, "Oh gaffer, it wath unbelievable, he'th bent it right into the pothtage thtamp." Now that was enough for me, I'm nearly gone already and my shoulders are heaving, but I say, "Tell them who scored it though Scalls." and out comes the reply, "Bathtian Thweinthteiger gaffer, Thweinthteiger curled it right in the pothtage thtamp!" I've lost it at that point and I'm nearly on the floor, the others are pissing themselves laughing. Neil realises what I've done and shouts, "Dodds, you're an athhole!"

PAUL SHEERIN (ex-Inverness Caledonian Thistle)

Whenever people talk to me about my playing career, they inevitably bring up that incredible night in February 2000 which led to the famous *Sun* headline, 'SUPER CALEY GO BALISTIC CELTIC ARE ATROCIOUS'. That 3–1 win over Celtic at Parkhead in the Scottish Cup was of course quite a night, it raised the profile of the club – we'd only been on the go for five years at that time – and of all of us players. We were getting letters of congratulation and emails from all over the world, and we were happy to take the credit for what was then the biggest match in the club's history. I would never, ever play down that result; I know what it meant to everyone associated with Caley Thistle, but I would still have to say it doesn't rank as the best or most important night of my career. It was a superb win against all the odds, but football is about winning trophies, not individual matches, and we went out to Aberdeen in the next round. So, in the end, that victory at Celtic Park really counted for nothing, even if it seemed like a huge occasion at the time. It was amazing to be part of it all, that was a great team and a good bunch of lads, but it's all just memories. I can think of other matches that had more significance, and actually produced something.

One example would be when I was with St Johnstone, it was the second last game of the season, and we beat Morton 3–1 at McDiarmid Park in May 2009 to clinch promotion back up to the SPL for the first time in seven years – now that really meant something. And when I was Arbroath manager we thumped Montrose 4–1 to win the Third Division – a convincing win in a local derby to clinch the championship with a couple of games to spare. That really did mean so much to me, especially as it was the first time the club had ever won a title.

On the flip side, there was that horrible time with St Johnstone in 2007 when we had won the final game of the season at 4–3 at Hamilton, and had to wait for Gretna to finish their match up in Dingwall. They were running late against Ross County and we were left hanging on for ages waiting for the result. It was still 2–2, they had to win to go up instead of us, and then deep into stoppage time James Grady went and scored their winner. That was gut-wrenching, absolutely horrendous, such a kick in the teeth, but that was another example of a game that really mattered. I will never forget that night at Celtic with Caley Thistle, it was very special, of course it was, but in the end it didn't have that edge to it in the way that the other occasions I mentioned did.

NEIL SIMPSON (ex-Aberdeen)

We were in Benidorm pre-season with Aberdeen, and inevitably the boys get a bit bored on occasion. Neale Cooper and John Hewitt were sharing a bedroom on the fifth floor, and decided to drop a football from the window to see how high it would bounce back up again. So they hung out, and let it go, the ball caught the edge of the swimming pool and rebounded over the perimeter fence never to be seen again. When we got our payslips in at the end of the week all the boys had been docked three pounds each without warning. It turned out Alex Ferguson and Archie Knox had been sitting by the pool and had seen the whole thing unfold, and we each got a copy of this poem, written by the boss, to remind us of our responsibilities . . .

 **The Aberdeen Football Club Ltd.**

PITTODRIE STADIUM, ABERDEEN AB2 1QH
telephone   6 3 2 3 2 8

Our Ref.

Your Ref.

You'll notice by your wage cheque
that I've fined you three pounds
For bouncing a ball from the tenth
floor into the Hotel grounds.

I know you won't like it
and are most probably sick
But please don't blame me
it was the one who performed this trick.

By now you will realise that I am very much aware
of anyone as stupid as to repeat this affair
So before you decide to get up to more pranks
The next time believe me, it will be no cheque in the Bank.

Signed by.................. *A. Ferguson.* ....
                    Poet Laureate of Govan

JIM DUFFY (ex-Dundee manager)

Dundee have had some pretty colourful owners and characters over the years and I worked with a few of them during my various spells as both player and manager. I was first in charge in the early- to mid-1990s and that was when I came across the larger-than-life Ron Dixon. He'd bought over the club before I arrived and had made all sorts of statements about challenging the Old Firm and about transforming and reconstructing Dens Park, but a greyhound racing track around the pitch seemed to be about the extent of what had materialised. I was up in the main stand one day and he came bustling over to me: "Jimmy, if those items aren't removed when I come back from my meeting they're going in the skip." I looked at the pitch, then turned back to him and said, "Those are the goalposts Mr Chairman." He was unmoved. "I don't care what they are Jimmy, they're making the dog track look untidy. I want them out of here." So, I had to get Brian the groundsman to lift them out and sit them in the stands behind the goals, otherwise we'd have had a few problems for the next match.

Another time I went to ask him to sign a purchase order for twenty footballs at fifty pounds each. We needed them for training and they were always ordered from the Scottish FA. He looked at it, questioned it, and after I'd explained the situation, said, "Fifty bucks for footballs? I've just seen them in the filling station for four bucks each!" I tried to point out that we needed more specialised equipment than might be sold in the local garage, but he was having none of it, and he called over the kit-man, gave him £100, and told him to go and buy the balls from there. For the hell of it, and because it was such a ridiculous scenario, we then carried out a full training session using beach balls, children's balls, balls of every colour and style imaginable. As you might expect, they were flying everywhere, it was a complete shambles. I waited until he'd gone for the day and then got the vice chairman, Malcolm Reid, to sign the order and sent it off to the SFA.

My second spell as manager came in the wake of the Bonetti brothers and the signings of the likes of Fabian Caballero and Claudio Caniggia. It also brought me into contact with the infamous Giovanni di Stefano, who has various convictions for fraud and spent many years pretending to be a qualified lawyer. He decided to put his legal 'qualification' to practical use one day at Hampden where we had a hearing involving Rangers over a contractual dispute regarding the defender Zurab Khizanishvili. He had moved to Ibrox and we wanted a transfer fee, while Rangers felt no money was owed. It was a high-profile case and they had a high-powered team of legal representatives there, while we had di Stefano. He stood up to make his opening remarks and said, 'The main point here is that clubs like Rangers can't go treating clubs like Dundee United in this way.' I did a double take on hearing that, while there were sniggers from the others in the room. That didn't augur well for our case and I immediately thought, 'Well, we're not winning this one'. What chance do you have when your own legal counsel can't even get the name of your club right? As expected, Rangers got the player on a free transfer. It was a tumultuous period to say the least.

One day after training I returned to Dens and Davie Provan was just emerging having interviewed di Stefano for Sky Sports. "Is he the full shilling?" he asked me, and when I shook my head, he said, "He's just told me you're going to be signing Edgar Davids." To say I was stunned would be something of an understatement! So, I went to see Giovanni and he claimed it had all been sorted with Davids – who was on £90,000 a week net at that time – and that all I had to do was go over to Turin to convince him to come. The Dutchman was one of the best play-ers in the world at that time, one of the biggest names in the game and at the peak of his powers. The thought of him signing for Dundee was just too ridiculous for words, and this bizarre scenario played out in my mind; "So Edgar, I know you're pre-paring for a vital Serie A encounter with Inter Milan, but we've got a Forfarshire Cup-tie with Brechin on Tuesday night, do you fancy playing in that instead? I know you're used to the best of facilities at this multi-million pounds training complex on the outskirts of the city, but we train three times a week at the Caird Park, and twice at the Michelin factory, fancy joining us?" That was one trip I never did make.

ERIC BLACK (ex-Birmingham City assistant manager)
The club had been the subject of a bid by the businessman Carson Yeung and the prospective new Chinese owners were touring the facilities. They wanted to see the manager, Steve Bruce, and we were told to report to the canteen after training. We're there on time, getting ourselves a coffee, when the door opens and eight of them walk in and sit around a table at the other end of the room. Steve and I stroll over and introduce ourselves and we take a seat ready for the questioning. Yeung asks a few, all very simple and straightforward enough, and Steve readily replies. At that point, a little guy sitting three seats away suddenly pipes up, "Why you not play Sutton up front?" Steve is a bit taken aback, but explains that we've been hit by a real injury crisis, that he's had to assess the personnel at his disposal, and that having gone through the squad, he decided that Chris would be best suited to the midfield role, which he felt he had adapted to really well in recent matches. It was a full and convincing assessment of the situation. The guy's expression doesn't change and he then asks, "Why Forssell not scoring goals?" I glance at Steve and I can see he's getting a bit twitchy, but he composes himself and responds politely, explaining that strikers go through such spells, that Mikael had been suffering a dip in confidence, but that he was convinced that would change and that he still had total belief in the player. This went on for a good few minutes with the guy asking about team tactics and selection, and Steve was clearly getting rattled. Eventually he'd had enough: "I'm sorry, I missed out on the introductions. Who are you?" The wee guy looked up

and said, "Me driver." I was under the table with laughter and Steve was ready to explode. I thought he might throw the guy through the canteen window, so I said we had a meeting with the players and I guided him out of there as quickly as I could.

IAN MAXWELL (Partick Thistle managing director)
Conrad Balatoni had been on loan with us from Hearts and had done really well. At the end of the season he was offered a full-time contract as we wanted to sign him on a permanent basis, and we quickly came to an agreement. Now Conrad's a smashing guy, and a good player, but he's maybe not the brightest. I've given him the forms to fill out, all the usual paperwork, and of course we need his bank details so we can pay his wages. He's sitting at my desk looking at them and it's taking a while. Eventually he looks up at me: "It says account holder?" and I explain, "Yes Conrad, that's you." He looks down again, thinks for a moment, and asks, "Is that Y.O.U?"

ALEX SMITH (ex-Clyde manager)
Season 1992–93 was a really tough one. It was before the move to the new stadium in Cumbernauld, so we worked out of Douglas Park in Hamilton, and it was a real battle with Brechin City and Stranraer in the Second Division. We eventually won the league title by a single point and got promoted, and that was such a relief.

As everyone knows, football has always been a big part of my life, maybe too big at times, but I do like to relax away from the game, to switch off. Music is one way I do that and my hero has always been Tony Bennett. I'd seen him a couple of times previously, but when I heard he was coming to the Royal Concert Hall in Glasgow I bought tickets for Janice and me thinking it would be the perfect way to wind down and celebrate after all the months of hard work. The night arrives and the great man steps on to the stage and immediately launches, unaccompanied, into Fly Me To The Moon and it was magnificent, he had the whole place spellbound. Beforehand we had gone for an Italian meal at a wee restaurant just round the corner, and as we were passing the back door of the building there's a big wine-coloured Rolls Royce sitting there. I look in and realise I know the chauffeur, he was a lovely guy, he used to drive all the dignitaries to Hampden, and so I say hello and he tells me he's just dropped the great man off, that I've just missed him. I tell the boy that I idolise Tony Bennett and he says, "Would you like to meet him? Just come round after the show and I'll sort it out for you." So all the way through the evening I'm sitting there feeling really excited, hoping I'm going to meet my hero, and when I go back out there's the chauffeur waiting for me. He guides me in along the corridor and I'm outside the dressing room. There's a big guy there, a burly security guard, standing in front of it and he recognises me and says, "Alex, how you doing?" and he opens the door. He stands to the side as the chauffeur walks me in and introduces me: "Mr Bennett, this is Alex Smith, he's a great fan of yours." Now, I can barely believe what's happening here as Tony Bennett greets me and shakes my hand, tells me that he's pleased to meet me. I'm star-struck.

Suddenly the big security guard pipes up, "Alex, tell him who you fucking are. Tell him who you are. Tell him you've just won the league championship with the Clyde!" I'm mortified, I'm blushing, but Tony Bennett starts laughing and asks, "Is this soccer?" So he starts congratulating me and asking about the team. I explain the club is named after the famous river in Glasgow and he insists we have a drink to celebrate. The security guard is loving this and he's calling over, "Tell him about the Clyde Alex, tell him about the Bully Wee!" It was such a bizarre night – here's me, a wee guy from Cowie meeting the legendary Tony Bennett, and you've got the boy shouting, "Tell him who you are!" That could only happen in Glasgow.

STEPHEN CRAIGAN (ex-Motherwell)

I think I have the unique distinction of having played in the three highest scoring matches in the history of the SPL, which for a centre-half isn't exactly something to be proud of!* Having now retired, I can look back and laugh at that but it didn't seem quite so funny at the time.

There was a nine-goal thriller with Dundee United in 2005, and that one started well enough as we were 2–0 up early on, and 3–1 up into the second half. Then the roof caved in and they scored three times in quick succession late on for a 5–4 victory. I went two goals better – or worse, I suppose – some years earlier in a ridiculous 6–5 defeat against Aberdeen in October 1999. Robbie Winters and John Spencer both scored hat-tricks that night, and what made it even more remarkable was that two of Scotland's best ever goalkeepers, Andy Goram and Jim Leighton, were at opposite ends of the pitch! They were 3–1 ahead by midway through the first half, and it was mayhem. It was 4–2 at half-time, then 6–4 with still twenty minutes left. It could have been anything that night! We got one back from the penalty spot, but despite throwing everything at them, couldn't get the equaliser. I'd actually started on the bench, but had been put on to replace Michel Doesburg after just ten minutes. Given that they were already 2–0 up by then, I always suspected he sensed what was in the offing and decided to have a convenient 'injury'!

I couldn't have imagined I would ever again be involved in a match quite like that, but towards the end of the 2009–10 season I played in the most incredible game I ever experienced in my

---

* The Scottish Premier League (SPL) ran from season 1998–99 until the end of 2012–13 and in the fifteen seasons it operated, the 6–6 and 6–5 matches Stephen mentioned were indeed the two highest aggregate scores during that time. Over the piece, six games produced nine-goal totals, Motherwell's 5–4 defeat to Dundee United being one of those, so there is some justification to Stephen's claim to fame!

whole career. Hibs scored first, we equalised, but Colin Nish got a hat-trick and by the break they were 4–2 up with John Sutton having scored just before it to give us some hope. Anthony Stokes got two quick goals for them though, and we were shell-shocked. After the second of them, Mark (Reynolds) turned to me and asked, "Is that five or six?" I honestly couldn't remember and had to look up at the scoreboard to check. Honestly, at that stage I'd have settled for eight – if someone had said stop now, eight conceded, I'd have taken it.

Things were looking that bad. But soon after, we had a free kick and while we were waiting for it to be taken, Ian Murray (Hibernian midfielder) said to me, "By the way, score this and you've still got a right chance!" Given that it was 6–2 at that time, I thought we had no chance, but they'd lost six in a row going into the game and their confidence was I suppose fragile. We scored, and a few minutes later I went up for another corner and he said, "Told you so. We can't defend." Given that we'd already conceded six that made me laugh. We scored from that one, then John Sutton got another, so that was 6–5 with fifteen minutes still to go, and we laid siege on their goal. With just a couple of minutes left we won a penalty.

Ross Forbes had only been on a few minutes, but he was confident, so stepped up to take it, and it was saved by Graeme Smith. That was devastating given how strongly we'd battled back, but deep into stoppage time Lukas Jutkiewicz lashed in an unstoppable volley to tie it all up. Six-six! Incredible!

I wandered off the park in something of a daze, I felt really deflated, and the manager, Craig Brown, came across and asked, "What happened there?" I looked at him, thought for a moment, and replied, "I've got no idea. To be honest, it's all a bit of a blur." He shook his head, looking as stunned as I felt, and said, "Maybe it's best staying as a blur. Let's just leave it at that." And he walked off.

DEREK McINNES (Aberdeen manager)

Man management is so important, it's one of the key parts of the job, and it's a way of getting your players to respect you and to go along with decisions you make. I worked under a number of guys who were excellent in that regard, but the one who fell really badly short was Dick Advocaat when he was at Rangers. He was brilliant with his starting eleven, he made no bones about what his best starting eleven was. He would say that's my best team, if they're fit, they play. His midfield was Barry Ferguson, Claudio Reyna and Giovanni van Bronckhorst, so that meant Jorg Albertz wouldn't play. Jorg would go and see him every week and get the same reply, 'I told you, if they're fit they play.'

There was one match where Barry and Giovanni had been out injured or suspended, and me and Charlie Miller played. He was magnificent, he scored, and he was all over the game, and the following week he wasn't even in the squad of nineteen and I only just made the bench. On that occasion Advocaat never even spoke to Charlie, never said 'you were excellent, you've given me food for thought for the future but I'm bringing the two boys back in because that's my team.' That's all he'd have needed to do, but he didn't, and of course at that point he's lost Charlie. He used to say to us we were well paid to be ready to play, and what he did to reinforce that was that every man in the squad of nineteen or twenty got the full bonus whether they played or not. So he recognised the importance of all the players in that respect, but he lacked that personal touch, and he got it wrong so often in how he handled us.

In 1999 I'd been away on loan at Stockport, came back, and he put me into the team for the Scottish Cup Final, a 1–0 win over Celtic. At the end of the game we're throwing him up in the air, giving it high-fives and having a huge celebration. Two weeks later I'm at home and Charlie Miller calls to say he's just had a letter from the club telling him he's no longer in the plans and that he's to report a week later than normal with Bomber's (John Brown) reserve team.

I'm sympathising with him and I hear the dog barking and I say, "Hold on, here's my postman" and sure enough, I've got the exact same letter! I couldn't believe it, I'd just played in the cup final a fortnight earlier, and now I'm being dumped by letter, he hasn't even had the decency to speak to me. In the end I knuckled down, got back in the side, played in the Champions League and got my move to Toulouse as a result of that. Before I left for France I went in to see him and told him how disrespectful I felt he'd been, that I'd never treat a player like that if I became a manager, and he said, "You know what McInnes, you're right, I shouldn't have handled it like that" and he wished me all the best, but by then I couldn't care less how he felt.

NEIL SIMPSON (ex-Aberdeen)
We used to do pre-season training at Gordonstoun School up near Elgin and on my first trip there I was only sixteen, and a bit naïve, just a young loon from Newmachar. Everyone else was wearing T-shirts and shorts at night, but I had my pin-stripe pyjamas, and as we were in a dormitory with five beds, they were quickly noticed. Word obviously spread, as lots of the other guys were dropping by to say goodnight and they're all going away sniggering.

Next morning, I fold up my jammies neatly and place them carefully under my pillow, then head away for training. Night-time comes, I lift my pillow, and they're gone. I spend the whole week asking who's got them, every evening, every day as we're lining up for sprints, as we're sitting down for food, I'm telling the guys I'm freezing at night, that I need my jammies back. The final afternoon we're walking back up to the dormitory blocks from the pitches and Stuart Kennedy wanders across to me. "Do you want to know where your pyjamas are?" I say yes, and he points up towards the roof of the school. They'd been flying from the flagpole the whole week and I'd never noticed them. Lesson learned; it was shorts and a T-shirt every year after that!

197

DAVID VAN ZANTEN (ex-St Mirren)

At the start of each season a senior police officer goes round all the clubs and does a speech, reading out the rules regarding players' behaviour on the pitch and how that might affect the fans. We were all gathered in the dressing room and there was a large wooden box there from the gym. It had a hole in it, and before the policeman came through I jumped into it and the lads placed a towel over the hole. When he arrived he stood right beside the box, took off his police hat, and placed it on the towel, completely unaware he'd put it right on top of my head. As he began talking the lads could see the hat beginning to move and of course they started sniggering. I could hear them, so started moving my head more, and then began making random noises from inside the box. The laughing grew louder and I could hear the officer was becoming a little unnerved, his voice sounding more and more awkward. This went on for a good three or four minutes, and as it was hot in there, the sweat was running down my face. I started making louder noises, and the laughing grew louder, before he eventually finished, picked up his hat and left the room. The manager, Danny Lennon, had no idea I was in the box and when he asked the boys why they'd been so amused, I jumped up and he nearly shit himself. He saw the funny side, but then realised he'd better go to explain to the policeman and dashed off after him. A year later it was a different officer and we tried the same trick, but when he came in he lifted the towel and said, "I've been warned about you!" Even now if I'm with any of the guys, someone just needs to say, "Remember that box?" and we're in fits of laughter.

ALASDAIR ROSS (assistant referee)

The last Old Firm game at Celtic Park before Rangers had their troubles, I was on the line and beforehand we got a knock on the door from Sky TV to say we're ready, you'll need to get the players in the tunnel. I was in charge of the away team, so I make my way along to the Rangers dressing room and the players are still coming in from their warm-up. I tell Ally McCoist that we need to go and he says he can't as he hasn't given his team-talk yet. I tell him we have to, Sky are ready, and he says he's got to talk to his players, he can't send then out without doing so. I told him he could have twenty-five seconds, so he grabbed my arm, closed the door and did his team-talk holding on to me. Not that it did much good as they went out and lost 3–0!

DEREK ADAMS (ex-Ross County)

We came back into the dressing room when I was with County, we'd lost, put in a shocking performance, and the manager Neale Cooper is going absolutely mental. He's had a go at everybody, he's punched the tactics board, the treatment table, he's lashing out at anything he sees. There's a black bin bag lying there, it's fully of dirty kit from the warm-up, so he kicks out at it and this bag arcs up across the room and lands straight on my head. I just sit there, I don't move, and big Cooper's still going on, he's shouting and bawling, I can hear him but I can't see him, and I'm trying to decide whether to take it off, or leave it there. This goes on for a few minutes longer, he's still going absolutely crazy, and I decide finally to remove it, and just as I do he's had enough and goes to storm out of the room. He grabs the handle, goes to pull it, and just about wrenches his arm out of his socket because somebody's locked the door! At that point we just all dissolved into laughter.

BILLY STARK (ex-Aberdeen)

Neale Cooper and Ian Angus had been injured and the routine at Aberdeen was you went in early for treatment, the rest of the boys went training, and you were then supposed to use the wee multi-gym, which was essentially a column with four exercise machines around it. It just so happened there was a full-size snooker table in the same room, and inevitably the boys would do a few routines then get a game of snooker going. The big risk was of course getting caught by Alex Ferguson, but you usually got a warning as he had this wee nervous cough and you could hear him coming along the corridor. 'Tattie' (Cooper) wants to play a frame and he's trying to persuade 'Og' (Angus), who's a quiet boy and says no, as he doesn't want to incur the manager's wrath, but eventually Cooper coaxes him into it. They're half-way through the first game when they suddenly hear the cough and 'Tattie' jumps on to the multi-gym and grabs hold of the equipment, but Ian freezes, he's petrified. The door opens, and Sir Alex is standing there. There's a moment's silence, Angus is like a rabbit in the headlights, and then he takes the snooker cue in both hands and starts pumping it above his head as if he's weightlifting. The manager was not best pleased!

DAVID VAN ZANTEN (ex-Hibernian)
I used to travel through to training in Edinburgh each day with John Rankin and as it was quite a long journey, we'd get a bit bored at times and be looking for a bit of fun. One of John's friends had been out at the weekend, had met and got chatting to a girl called Kylie, and although nothing had happened between them, the guy had fallen in love with her. John suggested I text his mate pretending to be the girl, to say that I'd got his number from a mutual friend, and to tell him how much I'd enjoyed his company. I fired off the text and there was an almost immediate reply. This continued over the next few days, the lad convinced he was chatting with Kylie, and as each reply came through I'd forward it to John and he'd send it round all their pals. As you might imagine, the texts began to get a bit saucy after a while, and on John's prompting 'Kylie' suggested they meet at a pub in Airdrie for a drink. Ranks told all his mates and they got done up in fancy dress and gathered outside, waiting for me to text to say he was there. When the guy sent a message to say he was waiting for her, I gave them the go-ahead. As he was sipping on his pint,

the whole gang came rushing into the pub going crazy, but even that didn't alert him and he was shouting at them, "You lot, fuck off! Kylie's going to be here any minute!" The boys couldn't contain themselves, they were falling about the floor laughing, and he eventually realised he'd been done up. I met him at a wedding a while later, and to be fair, he had a laugh about it. Eventually!

DEREK ADAMS (ex-Motherwell)

January 2002, I'm with Motherwell and we've got a Scottish Cup tie at Dunfermline which we lose 3–1, we've been well beaten. Eric Black was the manager, Terry Butcher his assistant, and the pair are having a right go at the players. Our striker David Kelly felt they were being unfair, picking on the younger guys, and he said to leave them alone and to concentrate on the older, more experienced players. That was just the invitation big Terry needed, and he gets stuck in to Kelly, who gets up and starts mouthing back, and all of a sudden Butcher's trying to get across the treatment table in the middle of the room and then Kelly lunges forward to try to get to him. Roberto Martinez, who was playing with us at the time, tries to stop it, the manager tries to stop it, and it becomes a melee, we're all involved, punches are being thrown, it's complete and utter chaos! We went back to Fir Park afterwards and had a team meeting to try to sort things out, and by Monday David Kelly was off, never kicked a ball for Motherwell again.

IAN MAXWELL (ex-St Johnstone)

It was pre-season and our striker, Keigan Parker, had turned his ankle during training. It wasn't anything serious, but the physio, Nick Summersgill, checked him out and gave him an ibuprofen tablet for the pain. We'd all gone up for lunch, it was laid out and we just helped ourselves, and then sat down to eat. Keigan pulls up a chair, cuts open a bread roll, puts the tablet inside, closes it again and takes a bite. One of the boys notices, bursts out laughing, and asks if he's just seen what he thinks he has, and serious as anything Keigan says, "What? Nick told me to take my pill with my lunch."

NEIL SIMPSON (ex-Aberdeen)
My time at Aberdeen coincided with the most successful period in the club's history when we won trophies season after season at home and in Europe, but it's amazing to think back at what we achieved despite the basic training facilities on offer to the players. One example of just how ridiculous it could be came when Ian Porterfield was in charge, having taken over from the legendary Alex Ferguson. There had been heavy snow overnight and it was lying quite thickly, so we couldn't train down at Seaton Park, which was one of our regular venues. Teddy Scott phoned round all the schools and local gymnasiums to see if we could book into one of them, but there's nothing free at all. All this time the whole first team squad has been hanging around just waiting to hear where we're going, and eventually the manager comes into the dressing room and says that we're just going to train down at the beach. There's about thirty of us, we get dressed up for the elements, and we all trudge out the front door through the snow and down the wee lane that runs alongside the golf course. At the end of it there's a tunnel, and we emerge at the top, just above the beach, to find the North Sea lapping at our feet; nobody had thought to check if the tide was in. It's incredible to think back to that, how unprofessional it could be. "Right lads, back to the stadium," says the manager, and we got an orange ball and trained in the snow on the car park across from the ground.

To be honest, this chapter could have gone on and on and on . . .

Football is big business these days and we can all be guilty of taking it too seriously at times; that's what the game does to us fans, and certainly does to managers, coaches and players. It grips us, it envelops us, it becomes all-consuming, and so it's hardly surprising that humour – quite often of the extremely black nature – plays such a huge part in the game.

The jokes, the wind-ups, the ridiculous and at times insane reactions to otherwise inconsequential incidents are, as much as anything, a way of coping with the day-to-day pressures and the often unforgiving environments of the training grounds and dressing rooms.

As has been evident in the pages you have just read, nothing is sacred, no one is safe, and no occurrence should be deemed too unlikely.

In Scottish football there seems to be just the one certainty . . . Anything can, and will, happen and when it does, it will be accompanied by howls of laughter.

ACKNOWLEDGEMENTS

So many people played their part in helping to get this book to the point where it could actually be published, and I would like to offer heartfelt thanks to each and every one of them.

Top of the list is the national team manager, Gordon Strachan, who came up with the idea as we worked on his foreword for my previous book, *Scotland 74: A World Cup Story*. As we chatted over a cup of tea in the Hampden cafe, Gordon, as he so often does, was regaling me with all sorts of amusing, incredible and ridiculous tales. He eventually paused, shook his head and chuckled, then said, "You know, someone should write a book with all these stories, I'd like to read that." Well, someone now has.

Thanks to all at Black & White Publishing, particularly Campbell Brown, who cajoled me into writing it early in 2015 when I was in need of a nudge.

My agent, Kevin Pocklington, also deserves a pat on the back for his continuing support and encouragement.

Most of all though, a huge and sincere thank you to all those from within the game, especially the players, coaches and officials past and present, who gave of their time willingly and shared some brilliant stories. No one declined to help, and while some took a bit longer to pin down, and others a bit of encouragement in recalling certain events, I hope you will agree it was well worth the seemingly never-ending stream of calls, texts and sit-down chats to assemble the collection of tales you have just read.

So, in alphabetical order, a big thanks to . . .

Derek Adams, Eric Black, Pat Bonner, Scott Booth, Dave Bowman, Billy Brown, Craig Brown, Terry Butcher, Jimmy Calderwood, Kenny Clark, Neale Cooper, Stephen Craigan, Callum Davidson, Billy Dodds, Jim Duffy, Derek Ferguson, John Hewitt, Peter Houston, Stuart Kennedy, Jim Leighton, Stuart McCall, Mark McGhee, Derek McInnes, Alex McLeish, John McMaster, Lee Mair, Ian Maxwell, Willie Miller, Campbell Money, Pat Nevin, Jimmy Nicholl, Craig Paterson, Allan Preston, Alasdair Ross, Duncan Shearer, Paul Sheerin, Neil Simpson, Alex Smith, Billy Stark, Gordon Strachan, Steven Thompson, Steve Tosh, Alex Totten, David van Zanten, Barry Wilson, Tommy Wright, Willie Young, and last but not least, my (very) old pal, Chick Young.

REFERENCE MATERIAL

While much of the book was put together using the quotes and recollections of the individuals who feature in it, some considerable research was required on occasion to verify or clarify certain memories. It has become clear to me in recent years that football players, in general, are terrible at remembering details of matches they have been involved in, or indeed, in some cases, whether or not they actually even played in a particular game.

In addition to filling in the blanks, I required to do some homework on the origins and historical development of the dugout, and on the individuals whose contribution led to separate chapters.

The afcheritage.org website was of considerable assistance throughout the writing process, along with other online sources.